Water Supply and Sanitation Services for the Rural Poor

Water Supply and Sanitation Services for the Rural Poor – The Gram Vikas Experience

Pamela Keirns

PRACTICAL ACTION
Publishing

Published by Intermediate Technology Publications Ltd
trading as Practical Action Publishing
Schumacher Centre for Technology and Development
Bourton on Dunsmore, Rugby
Warwickshire CV23 9QZ, UK
www.practicalactionpublishing.org

© Institute of Development Studies, 2007

First published in 2007

ISBN 978 1 85339 654 0

A catalogue record for this book is available from the British Library.

The contributors have asserted their rights under the Copyright
Designs and Patents Act 1988 to be identified as authors of their
respective contributions.

Since 1974, Practical Action Publishing has published and disseminated
books and information in support of international development work
throughout the world. Practical Action Publishing (formerly ITDG
Publishing) is a trading name of Intermediate Technology Publications Ltd
(Company Reg. No. 1159018), the wholly owned publishing company of
Intermediate Technology Development Group Ltd (working name Practical
Action). Practical Action Publishing trades only in support of its parent
charity objectives and any profits are covenanted back to Practical Action
(Charity Reg. No. 247257, Group VAT Registration No. 880 9924 76).

Cover design by Mercer Online
Typeset by S.J.I. Services
Index preparation: Indexing Specialists (UK) Ltd
Printed by Replika Press

Contents

Boxes

Figures

Photos

Maps

Tables

Abbreviations and acronyms

ADB	Asian Development Bank
adivasi	Oriya word for inhabitants from prehistoric times, the indigenous tribal people of India. Most Hindu-Indians see *adivasi* as lower in status than themselves. In the Constitution of India they are referred to as Scheduled Tribe (ST).
APL	above poverty line
ARWSP	Accelerated Rural Water Supply System
BPL	below poverty line. GoI's definition of the poverty line is having income high enough for adequate nutrition.
CBO(s)	community-based organization(s)
CRSP	Central Rural Sanitation Programme
CSO	civil society organization
CVC	Clean Village Campaign
dalit	Oppressed or Downtrodden, those below the lowest level of the Hindu caste system. Other castes are usually not interested in the opinion of *dalit* and often they have no access to the village temple or the best water source. In the Constitution of India they are referred to as Scheduled Caste (SC). They were termed 'untouchables' in the caste system; Gandhi called them *harijan* (Children of God); their own leaders called them *dalit* or *bahujan* in a rights movement in the 1980s.
DC	District Collector
DDWS	Department of Drinking Water Supply (part of Ministry of Rural Development, GoI)
DFID	Department for International Development, UK government ministry
Empowerment	Ensuring that the powerless (marginalized women, the poor and other groups) are given a voice, and increasing their capacity to participate in community decision-making (Moriarty and Butterworth, 2003).
GC	General Caste
GoI	Government of India
GoM	Government of Maharashtra
GP	*gram panchayat* (village council), lowest tier of local government
IEC	information, education and communication
INR	Indian rupees. INR100=US$2.48=£1.25 at 1 June 2007
ITDP	Integrated Tribal Development Programme

JMP WHO/UNICEF Joint Monitoring Programme for Water Supply and Sanitation

MANTRA Movement and Action Network for Transformation of Rural Areas, Gram Vikas's habitats programme which integrates the ITDP and RHEP approaches

MDG(s) Millennium Development Goal(s)

MoU Memorandum of Understanding

MPR monthly progress report

NGO(s) non-government organization(s). In this report the term refers to voluntary organizations specializing in social development work in poor communities.

Nirmal Gram (Clean Village Award), a GoI cash incentive scheme for
Puraskar fully sanitized villages

ODI Overseas Development Institute

O&M Operation and Maintenance, e.g. electricity charges for pumping, pump operator's wages, spare parts

panchayat village-level elected body

panchayati raj constitutional system of local self-governance

PBO project beneficiary organization

PMED planning, monitoring, evaluation and documentation

PRI(s) *panchayat raj* institution(s), local government institution(s) (see Box 2.2)

RHEP Rural Health and Environment Programme, water and sanitation aspect of Gram Vikas's MANTRA

SC Scheduled Caste: the term used in the Constitution of India to refer to *dalit*

SDC Swiss Agency for Development and Cooperation, Swiss government ministry

SHG(s) self-help group(s)

ST Scheduled Tribe: the term used in the Constitution of India to refer to *adivasi*

Swajaldhara GoI's rural water-supply programme

TSC Total Sanitation Campaign, GoI's main sanitation programme

UN United Nations

UNICEF United Nations Children's Fund

VEC village executive committee

VERC village education resource centre

VSBK vertical shaft brick kiln

WAB WaterAid–Bangladesh

WAI WaterAid–India

WASH Water Supply and Sanitation Collaborative Council's WASH (Water Sanitation and Hygiene for all) Campaign

WASIO WaterAid South India Office

WELL	resource centre network which provides access to information and support in water sanitation and environmental health and related issues in developing and transitional countries. Website: http://www.lboro.ac.uk/well/index.htm
WHO	World Health Organization
WSP–SA	Water and Sanitation Program–South Asia

Preface

Gram Vikas is a secular non-government organization (NGO), working in the rural development sector in Orissa, India. [In Hindi (and Oriya), *gram* means village and *vikas* means development.] The organization has worked with poor and marginalized communities of Orissa since 1979, aiming to make sustainable improvements in the quality of life of the rural poor. Its interventions are directed at raising critical consciousness and energizing whole villages. Through their Rural Health and Environment Programme (RHEP) intervention, Gram Vikas uses water and sanitation as the entry-point for creating unity and enabling communities to start their own development. All of its work is governed by five core values: social equity, inclusion, gender equity, cost-sharing and sustainability.

'It wasn't this easy before,' says Manu, describing her life in her native village, Khatuakuda in the Ganjam district, Orissa, India. Manu is one of the key instigators in bringing about change in her village: getting clean piped drinking water to every household, and individual toilets and bathing rooms for each family. Prior to this they got water from a well in the next village, over half an hour's walk away. Manu's day used to start at 3.00 am, and for four hours in the morning and two hours in the evening she would balance the large water pots upon her head for endless trips to and from the well. For big events like weddings women would spend the whole day before just collecting water – 'and everyone was forever getting married!' says Manu, 'often we would not be looking forward to the festivities at all.' One day, after spraining her ankle, she decided she had had enough. Manu rallied the women. Together they convinced the village of the need for water supply through taps at their individual homes, and toilets and bathing rooms as an alternative to trekking through swampy marshlands every time they wanted to relieve themselves. They approached Gram Vikas for assistance with implementing their RHEP in Khatuakuda. The women of Khatuakuda pushed the programme from one stage to the next, and acted as the main organisers and collectors for the community contribution to the project. Even now, after the construction of water and sanitation infrastructure is completed, Manu is still busy with her Self-Help Group (SHG) planning the next project – 'There's always much more to be done,' she says. She explains that the access road to the village needs repair, and with the help of Gram Vikas they are now lobbying for government funds. Manu's SHG also provides her with support and the confidence to send her daughter to school, a contentious issue with her mother-in-law. 'I want my daughter to go all the way ... I don't want her to be just a housewife.'

A visit to some of the other rural villages in which Gram Vikas has implemented the RHEP makes three things clear: the people are really proud of their achievements; they have a clear vision for the future; and the process of change, once begun, gathers momentum and affects different aspects of the villagers' lives. They all admit that Gram Vikas's initiatives have changed their lives. In Samiapalli, villagers proudly display their well-arranged houses and sanitary blocks with piped water, the water tower, the neat drainage lanes, the social forestry patches and the village pond. The constant comparison is to the town of Berhampur nearby. Annapurna Reddy in Mathamukundapur says, 'We used to step out of our houses into six inches of muck. Now look around – everything is so clean. There's running water in the house.' In Samantrapur, the villagers show off their 1300 sq ft community hall. In this village, the executive committee has started steering government programmes. 'Now even the government wants to invest in our village. They have invested INR300,000 [US$6,500] in the school building and the village road,' the villagers say.

The most talked about change in the villages is women's participation in community affairs; this involvement of women has led to increased levels of confidence. Annapurna Reddy is convinced that the fact that women have access to their own money through their savings schemes has changed the social equation. Village women are still expected to be in purdah, but even that is slowly changing in RHEP villages. In Suryanarayanpur, both men and women will tell you that purdah not only covers the face but the mind also. In the past the women of Kusagumma were no different from other rural women of southern Orissa: age-old traditional conservatism had made them stay indoors, unable to speak up for themselves, covering their faces behind veils. They were not educated; nor were they given any opportunity to express themselves or take part in community decision-making, other than taking care of the family and assisting in agriculture. Now they are using their spare time (saved by not having to fetch water) to learn to read and write through their SHG's support and to participate in community work. Now they share the same community platform with men, make decisions and implement them. Men now encourage the women's endeavours, treat them with more respect and realize the importance of educating girls. Not all the women in Kusagumma, however, are convinced. They still think that the younger women, the daughters-in-law, need not step out of the house 'unnecessarily'. But village meetings are already seen as 'necessary' outside appearances and it is only a matter of time before other events are also seen as necessary for women to attend. There is a widespread belief among villagers that united community action can make a huge difference.

'Few development projects successfully address quality of life and long-term sustainability issues ... there are even fewer examples of sustainable projects that focus on the ... marginalized sections of society. [Gram Vikas's] RHEP is such a programme. It uses development funds only as seed money to catalyze a change in the rural economy by generating and regenerating local resources' (Swiss Agency for Development and Cooperation [SDC], 2000). Real success stories in the development sector are seldom publicized because of a lack of documentation. This lack of publicity means that the fundamental changes that the successful programme is bringing about are not fully communicated to other development practitioners, or to potential donors and financiers; valuable insight is lost to the sector and the programme cannot possibly scale up to its full potential; the real losers are those living in the underdeveloped regions of the world. Gram Vikas's sustainable, community-oriented development process needs to be shared across the development sector so that the lessons can be implemented on as wide a scale as possible. That is the purpose of this publication.

CHAPTER 1

Water and sanitation – breaking the poverty cycle

This chapter starts by outlining the burden that the lack of water and sanitation places on poor people worldwide, and introduces the Millennium Development Goals (MDGs) for improving coverage. This is followed by an examination of the role that water and sanitation can play in the reduction of poverty. World Health Organization (WHO)/ UNICEF Joint Monitoring Programme (JMP) statistics relating to water and sanitation coverage worldwide are quoted, observing which regions have least coverage. This is followed by a brief examination of why coverage remains so low and a reflection on the implications for meeting the MDGs.

Introduction

'The combination of safe drinking water and hygienic sanitation facilities is a precondition for health and for success in the fight against poverty, hunger, child deaths and gender inequality.' (WHO, 2004)

Let us start with a few statistics.

- 10,000–20,000 people, mainly children, die every day from preventable water- and sanitation-related diarrhoeal diseases such as cholera and dysentery.
- At least 1.6 million children under the age of five die from these diseases every single year, which is more than eight times the number of people who died in the Asian tsunami of 2004 (WHO, 2006).
- At the beginning of 2005, 1.1 billion people (a sixth of the world population) did not have access to clean drinking water; and 2.6 billion people (that is, about a third of the world population, or one in three people) did not use a toilet but defecated in the open or in unsanitary places.

There is a direct relationship between water, sanitation and health. Poor sanitary conditions lead to the contamination of water bodies and the general environment, including crop land. Practices such as open defecation, unhygienic behaviour (e.g. not washing hands before touching food) and haphazard waste disposal are common in developing countries in all regions of the world (Kar, 2003), leaving people exposed to bacterial diseases like diarrhoeas, dysenteries and typhoid, as well as parasitic worms. Unconfined human waste is also a breeding ground for insect vectors like cockroaches and flies which can increase the spread

---

Box 1.1 The specific MDG targets relating to water and sanitation

- To halve, by the year 2015, the proportion of people without sustainable access to adequate quantities of affordable and safe water.
- To halve, by the year 2015, the proportion of people without access to hygienic sanitation facilities (this target was added in 2002 after the Johannesburg World Summit).
- By 2025 to provide water, sanitation and hygiene for all.

Note that these figures are percentages; due to population growth (especially in cities), the capacity will have to be increased just to stand still, never mind increase coverage.

---

of excreted pathogens and eye infections. The undernourished, the very young and the elderly are particularly susceptible – epidemics frequently kill thousands. The simple act of washing hands with soap and water can reduce diarrhoeal diseases by over 40 per cent (WaterAid, undated). Not having enough water to wash properly often means that people suffer from skin diseases like scabies and eye infections such as trachoma, the largest cause of preventable blindness in the developing world.

Safe water and adequate sanitation are known to be vital for improving health and well-being, but they also link to poverty reduction through improved livelihoods, improved education and better quality of life (the next section will elaborate more on this). The international community has given a commitment, through the MDGs adopted by all member states of the United Nations (UN), to reduce worldwide poverty, inequality, hunger and illness over the next decade. It is widely acknowledged that investing in water, sanitation and hygiene is necessary if the MDGs on poverty reduction, education and health are to be met. With about 70 per cent of the world's poor living in rural areas, the Asian Development Bank (ADB, 2006) says, it is paramount that we attend to the issues of rural water and sanitation as a matter of urgency. 'This effort must be made, not only for humanitarian reasons, but also because it is highly cost-effective, reduces health costs enormously, and is directly related to health, equity and economic growth, which are prerequisites for poverty alleviation.' (WHO, 2006)

How water and sanitation projects can help to break the poverty cycle

Lack of adequate clean water and hygienic sanitation, and the diseases resulting from this lack, are a major cause of poverty in developing countries. Many organizations, such as WaterAid, WELL, the Water Supply and Sanitation Collaborative Council's WASH Campaign (Water Sanitation and Hygiene for all) and the Department for International Development (DFID), have reported on the benefits resulting from successful water, sanitation and hygiene projects. The following section is based on such reports.

The very poor, who are usually dependent on daily-wage labour for their income and survival, cannot afford to fall ill – their physical fitness is their main productive asset. If they do get sick, they cannot work and therefore earn no money. The very poor seldom have savings or access to credit, so medical bills must be met by loans, usually from moneylenders and at high interest rates. The result is that after recovering from the illness the family is in even deeper poverty. For individual households, a high incidence of disease may mean investing as much as 30 per cent of their income on health care, as found in a preliminary study in Thatta, Pakistan (Majumdar, 1994). These easily-preventable sicknesses also put severe strains on national health services and hospitals; 73 million working days are lost each year in India to waterborne diseases, at a cost of US$600m in terms of medical treatment and lost production (WaterAid, undated).

For much of the developing world fetching water is a daily chore. This is often considered to be women's work, but in many countries children, particularly girls, get this task; girls as young as 10 years old may take the main responsibility for drawing and carrying the family's water. Commonly several journeys have to be made to satisfy all the daily household needs and heavy containers of up to 20 kg have to be carried on each return journey.[1] In rural areas, depending on the distance to the nearest water source, this can mean a walk of several kilometres, perhaps through unsafe territory. In rural Africa women often walk 10 miles (16 km) or more every day to fetch water, and in the dry season it is not uncommon for women to walk twice this distance. As well as travelling such long distances, women often have to wait in turn to collect water; waiting times can add hours on to the journey. In Ethiopia, Somalia, Uganda and Tanzania many millions of women spend 40–50 minutes on each round trip (WHO, 2006). To avoid the queue women and children often get up in the middle of the night to fetch water. Not only is this an enormous drudgery – carrying such heavy loads can damage the head, neck and spine, and is especially difficult for women when they are pregnant or suffer from disease – but it also affects women's mental health, due to stress and lack of sleep. Having a clean water source close by means women can get their sleep, have lower stress levels and can spend more time with their families; they can wash themselves, their children and their homes, utensils and clothes more regularly; this all leads to a healthier, happier home. More time can be productively spent in income-generating activities and improving the economic status of the family.[2] Having water and better hygiene during pregnancy and childbirth means less risk of post-natal infections; women also report having fewer children when they know that children have a better chance of survival.

Increased education, particularly of girls, is accepted as a key means of breaking the cycle of poverty; the basic skills of reading, writing and arithmetic are important livelihood tools. 'Women with even a few years of basic education have smaller, healthier families; are more likely to be able to work their way out of poverty and are more likely to send their own children – both girls and boys – to school. Each additional year of female education is thought to reduce child mortality by 5–10 per cent' (WaterAid, undated). Less time spent carrying water means that children have more time to attend school (or play). Many children from poor families who do enrol for school often drop out because they are needed at home to help in farming or domestic chores or to care for the sick (this task frequently falls to a girl child). Improvement in health results in less absence of pupils from school, not only because the child itself falls ill less often, but also because it is being withdrawn from school less frequently to take on an ill parent's household and income-earning responsibilities.

In conservative societies, where women's modesty is of great importance and significance, open defecation presents a huge moral dilemma for many village women and adolescent girls, says Kar (2003). The absence of privacy for dealing with natural bodily functions and having to expose oneself in the open, especially during menstruation, affects women's dignity and sense of self-worth. Women face harassment while practising open defecation; in many areas they have few options for privacy during the daylight hours and must walk some distance in order to find a suitable place. To avoid that, they go to the fields to answer the call of nature only before sunrise or after sunset. This suppression of natural urges causes genito-urinary health problems, as Gram Vikas found in its village surveys. The lack of adequate sanitation facilities in schools also prevents girls from attending school, particularly when they are menstruating. Teachers also benefit from adequate water and sanitation and are more likely to want to work in schools that have better facilities.

Having more time to spend farming and planning for their futures has increased the resistance to drought and famine of communities in Ethiopia (WaterAid, undated). With water, and more time, people can grow kitchen gardens, more crops, or livestock; any excess over family needs can be sold at market. Having more vegetables and better food to eat means improved health and nutrition, increasing people's resistance to diseases, especially diarrhoea, pneumonia, measles and malaria.

Successful water and sanitation projects bring wider social benefits too. Deverill et al. say (2002) that the underlying causes of poverty are complex: an important factor is access to and control over resources, but some less obvious factors are exclusion and inequality on the basis of gender, ethnicity, religion, caste, politics and livelihood. In particular, women are often excluded from decision-making in the home and in the wider community. Involving women in making decisions for the implementation of their water and sanitation projects means that men

---

Box 1.2 Out from the depths

Before their water and sanitation project was implemented, Nakwetikya from Ndedo, Tanzania, used to have to collect the scarce water available, polluted with animal and human waste, from the bottom of deep and dangerous hand-dug pits. Sickness and deaths were common. 'The situation here used to be bleak,' she explains. 'There was no water and we had to dig pits to find some. Can you imagine what it was like? My legs used to shake with fear before climbing down those holes. There was no choice. If I didn't get water my family couldn't eat, wash or even have a drink. When I heard that we were going to get clean water I remember laughing, it was so funny. I can only compare it to someone who is in prison for a long time. When they are set free it's the most fantastic experience.

'Since having the new water source life has changed in so many amazing ways. My status as a woman has been finally recognized. I have the time to look after my family as we have more time and energy. Before we formed a committee and prepared ourselves as a community, men just saw women as animals. I think they thought of us as bats flapping around them. They had no respect for us and no one would allow you to speak, or listen to what you had to say. When I stand up now in a group I am not an animal, I am a woman with a valid opinion. We have been encouraged and trained and the whole community has learnt to understand us.'

Source: WaterAid (undated).

---

finally have to listen to them. Women benefit from more respect and raised self-esteem; they are involved more in domestic financial decision-making and political decisions. Involvement of other marginalized groups, such as the extremely poor, can help to raise their social status too. A core thrust of Gram Vikas's work is to involve the marginalized as well as women in all aspects of development, with the aim of raising the self-esteem of these groups so that they will claim that to which they are entitled.

For the community, the reduction in open defecation means a cleaner environment and generates a sense of civic pride; some people report no longer being ashamed to invite relatives and friends to visit. WaterAid reported (undated) that 'following projects that include training in maintenance, management, accounting and hygiene education, many communities report feeling a sense of cohesion, confidence and an ability to carry out work on their own. This enables the poorest communities in the world to plan further for their own futures.'

Global situation on access to water and sanitation

Information in this section is extracted from the JMP (WHO, 2006).

Water

As stated earlier, about a sixth of the world population – a total of 1.1 billion people – do not have access to safe drinking water. Despite huge efforts to increase coverage, because of population growth the number of people unserved has not changed substantially since 1990. Nearly 80 per cent of the unserved population is concentrated in three regions (see Figure 1.1): sub-Saharan Africa (322 million people), Southern Asia (206 million) and Eastern Asia (302 million). One out of every two persons unserved live in Southern Asia or Eastern Asia.

Coverage in rural areas lags far behind that in urban areas: 84 per cent of the unserved (some 900 million people) live in rural areas (see Figure 1.2). In almost the entire developing world coverage in rural areas

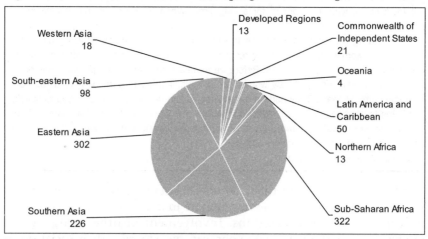

Figure 1.1 Total populations (m) without improved drinking water, 2004
Source: WHO, 2006 (figure 4).

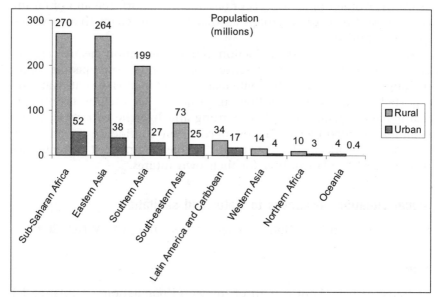

Figure 1.2 Rural and urban populations (m) without improved drinking water, 2004
Source: WHO, 2006 (figure 10).

remains unacceptably low at around 73 per cent, so that around one in four people do not have safe water. If the current trend in coverage continues, the JMP projects, in 2015 about 700 million will still not have safe drinking water.

A water connection at the house, drawing water from a public distribution system, is proven to give the greatest health benefits, because where householders have to walk more than 5 minutes to get their water, it is likely that they will not use more than the very minimal quantities required for hygiene, drinking and cooking. Only 44 per cent of the developing world's population has access to improved drinking water through a household connection; the other 36 per cent with access to improved water get it from wells, standpipes, etc. Again there is an urban–rural disparity: 70 per cent of the urban population in developing regions has household connections, only 25 per cent of the rural population has this type of service. There are also huge disparities between world regions, only 16–28 per cent of households are connected in sub-Saharan Africa, Southern Asia and South-eastern Asia having; most other regions have 70 per cent connected or higher.

Sanitation

One out of two people in developing regions – 2.6 billion people – has no access to improved sanitation; they are obliged to defecate in the open or use unsanitary facilities, with a serious risk of exposure to sanitation-related diseases. Again, because of population growth, the number of people unserved has not changed substantially since 1990. Over 80 per cent of the unserved population is concentrated in the familiar three regions (see Figure 1.3): sub-Saharan Africa (463 million),

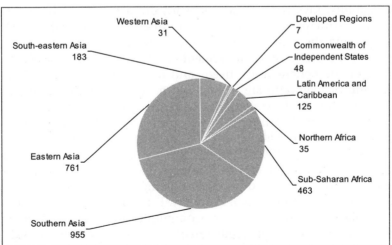

Figure 1.3 Total populations (m) without improved sanitation in 2004
Source: WHO, 2006 (figure 15).

Eastern Asia (761 million) and Southern Asia (955 million); coverage in these regions is a very low 37–45 per cent. Out of every three persons unserved, two live in Southern Asia or Eastern Asia.

Of the unserved, 611 million are urban dwellers and a staggering 2 billion (77 per cent) live in rural areas; 39 per cent of rural dwellers do not have access to improved sanitation. In most developing countries, rural populations are migrating to urban areas: from 2007 onwards, the world urban population will be greater than the rural population. Even taking this into consideration, the JMP predicts that in 2015 the number of unserved rural dwellers (1.7 billion) will still be more than twice the number of unserved urban residents (7 million). At the current rate of growth only 49 per cent of the rural population will have sanitation by 2015.

Why does coverage remain so low?

Although provision of water and sanitation in developing countries has been seen as a high priority need by the development community since the 1990s, not much headway has been made, especially in sanitation; why is this?

Many projects that were completed during the 1990s and earlier have proven unsustainable and fallen into disrepair. Development should involve cooperative planning and collaboration between government departments, attacking the issue using a multi-pronged approach both at local and national level, says the Overseas Development Institute (ODI, 2002). Sustainability needs to be considered from the very start of a project – institutional, financial, social, technical and environmental sustainability – if any long-term economic improvement is to be seen. Sustainability, says Gely (2006), depends on: a planning strategy that involves 'participation, consensus-building and coordination' (ODI, 2002) among the different stakeholders, and identifying mechanisms that will lead to effective management of water and sanitation; facilities that meet the beneficiaries' needs and preferences so that they take ownership of them and are willing and have the capacity to maintain them; operation and maintenance costs being met so that the system remains functional, prices for water and sanitation services set at a level that people are willing and able to finance so that the system is self-funding (Gely, 2006). Using local materials and labour when building and training locals to maintain the facility (e.g. hand-pump mechanics) have the added benefits of giving a sense of ownership and injecting money into the local economy. It is important to also educate the people in hygienic practices. Community involvement is a time-consuming practice that needs effective communication, so skilled communicators need to be part of the development team, something that has frequently been missing in the past, according to Gely.

The ADB says (2006) that the main reasons why the poor continue to lack access to safe water and sanitation are as follows.

- The sector remains one of the lowest priorities of government in terms of allocation of resources, in spite of the health and economic value attributed to safe water and adequate sanitation.
- The low priority accorded by governments to rural water and sanitation. When government does invest in the sector, the tendency is to package large-scale water and sanitation projects that focus on urban populations that are able to pay for higher levels of service at full cost-recovery water rates.
- Inefficient and inadequate government strategies to deliver sustained services, for example inadequate institutional arrangements, insufficient cost-recovery, poor operation and maintenance. At present, the ADB says, a national strategy to address the needs of the poorest of the poor remains lacking in most countries in the Asian region.

A Government of India (GoI) assessment of water and sanitation in India (2002b: 38) found that some of the issues that stood in the way of effective implementation of rural sanitation programmes included:

1. the very low priority given to sanitation by the state governments and the population in general;
2. low emphasis on information, education and communication (IEC);
3. lack of motivation efforts;
4. lack of community participation;
5. heavy reliance on subsidy; and
6. lack of NGO or private-sector involvement.

WaterAid–India (WAI) suggests (2006) that 'possibly a combination of all of [the following] factors is acting to inhibit construction and use of toilets in rural India': poverty, caste, gender and social exclusion, lack of water availability, nature of rural livelihoods and livelihoods insecurity.

It will be seen later in the book that from the beginning Gram Vikas has insisted on inclusion of all strands of society in their interventions, that is, all male and all female heads of household irrespective of caste or wealth. They have understood the need for the people to be fully involved in decision-making and sharing of costs relating to, and maintenance of, their infrastructure if service is to be sustained. This is outlined in Chapter 3 (p. 34 onwards) and is also described more fully in later sections. Gram Vikas spends a lot of time on educating villagers about the need for sanitation and motivating them to adopt hygienic practices, and in the development of livelihood strategies.

The implications for meeting the MDG targets

The WHO states (2006) that the world urgently needs to step up activities, increase effectiveness and accelerate investments if the MDG targets are to be met: a continuous and sustained development process is needed. Many least developed countries will have to more than double their efforts if they are to reach the drinking water target, and an intensive effort is needed to increase coverage in rural populations. To meet the sanitation target over 140 million people in developing regions need to gain access to improved sanitation annually until 2015 (Southern Asia, 51 million; sub-Saharan Africa, 35 million; Eastern Asia, 29 million). That is almost 384,000 people every day, a doubling of the current efforts. Rural sanitation, especially, requires a massive concentration of effort.

It is essential, says WHO (2006), to prevent current and future infrastructure falling into disrepair as a result of an overall lack of sound management practices. Investing in sanitation infrastructure involves a long project cycle and, if the MDG sanitation target is to be achieved, innovative approaches need to be developed to reduce the time span from policy-making to services delivery.

WAI (2005) makes the very important point that, while the numbers of people with water and sanitation may well increase significantly over the period to 2015, it does not necessarily follow that the poorest and neediest will benefit. If funds are channelled towards improvements that mainly benefit wealthier urban areas, the rural (and urban) poor are likely to lose out. Future development must try to overcome this inequity. India illustrates this point: the economy has seen rapid development in recent years, but that has not helped the rural poor very much. Much more effort has been made by the government to facilitate urban than rural development. The result is that remote areas have been severely neglected and further marginalized.

Gram Vikas has been successfully implementing sustainable rural water and sanitation projects, which focus on the poor and marginalized, since 1992. It has reached more than 150,000 people to date, and those people have continued to further develop their communities on their own initiative (as will be seen in Chapter 6, p. 72 onwards). Its Rural Health and Environment Programme (RHEP) process can certainly help to meet the MDGs in a sustainable and cost-effective fashion – the initial seed-capital which they inject is regenerated time and again in local resources – but perhaps more significantly it can help the poorest of the poor rural people, the most marginalized, to hold their heads high and start creating a different future for themselves.

CHAPTER 2
Water and sanitation in India

This chapter looks at the situation regarding water and sanitation coverage in India specifically, and the burden suffered due to related diseases. This is followed by an examination of the socio-economic context of Orissa (the Indian state in which Gram Vikas works) and the poor conditions in which most of the population lives. Government strategies for increasing water and sanitation coverage are outlined, as is the role that partner organizations can play.

The burden due to lack of sanitation and clean water

India is one of the most densely populated countries in the world, with a population of around 1.09 billion; 72 per cent of the population (around 782 million) is rural. The country has one of the lowest sanitation coverages in the world, at 33 per cent (WHO, 2006); people, generally speaking, have no knowledge of the importance of hygienic practices, and answer the call of nature wherever they see fit. Often they defecate beside the village pond, where there is a handy source of water for anal cleansing. In many villages in India that same pond is used for all water purposes: drinking water, and washing cattle, clothes and people.

The lack of availability of safe drinking water, and the lack of sanitation and solid waste disposal have been identified by the Government of India (GoI) as being the main reason for current ill health and morbidity levels in India. The World Bank reports (2003) that it is perhaps the principal cause of life-threatening diseases among infants and children. The GoI's Department of Drinking Water Supply says (DDWS, undated) that statistics show 30 million people on average in rural areas of India suffer from sanitation-related disease and about 0.4–0.5 million children die annually of diarrhoea.[3]

There is also 'indication of annual loss of 180 million man-days and INR12 bn to the economy owing to sanitation related diseases'. Females also suffer from gynaecological disorders and diseases such as scabies because modesty dictates that they have to remain fully clothed while washing themselves in public.

During the rainy season the number of sanitation-related diseases increases because run-off water washes faeces into the ponds. Also, fetching water or finding privacy for defecation is even more problematic than usual during the monsoon months because the slippery, muddy conditions make it difficult to walk far.

Access to water

According to the JMP, 83 per cent of rural households in India have protected water and 8 per cent have household connections (see Table 2.1). However, a joint WHO/UNICEF/Planning Commission GoI study (GoI, 2002b) found large variations in coverage levels between states. Statistics released by the DDWS indicate that 94 per cent of rural habitations were 'fully covered' by government water points in 2004 (WAI, 2005: 19).[4] The GoI's mid-term assessment report of their 10th Five-Year Plan stated that only 38 per cent of rural households have water in or near the home (GoI, 2005: 221).[5]

Irrespective of the precise coverage levels, independent studies have reported a scarcity of drinking water in about half of the villages in India (GoI, 2002a: 19). That is not too surprising when you consider the low design-allowance rate of the government schemes (40 litres per person per day), but the shortages may also be partly due to breakdowns, poor power supply or summer droughts. WAI reports (2005) that a large number of government water sources are non-functional or not used. Many rural dwellers in India still use nearby (unprotected) water sources rather than walk long distances to government water points; even in areas that are 'fully covered' (e.g. Uttar Pradesh and Bihar) large numbers of people suffer from water-related diseases because they still draw dirty water from private shallow wells. So, although the government considers these people to be 'fully covered', in effect they are not. Despite massive outlays, access to safe drinking water remains a challenge in rural India.

Access to sanitation

The JMP figures shown in Table 2.1 state that only 22 per cent of rural households in India have access to improved sanitation. WAI estimates (2005) that rural sanitation coverage countrywide is only about 15 per cent, and that few villages are free of open-defecation. It has been

Table 2.1 Access to improved drinking water and sanitation in India, %

Access to improved drinking water %						Access to improved sanitation %		
Countrywide		Urban		Rural		Country-wide	Urban	Rural
Total	Household connection	Total	Household connection	Total	Household connection			
86	19	95	47	83	8	33	59	22

Source: WHO, 2006.

estimated that 15,000 truckloads of human faeces are produced daily in India, and are left exposed (WSP–SA, 2002).

Again there are large inter-state variations in coverage, with larger, more populated and poorer states having much lower access rates than the national average; Orissa is at the bottom end with less than 10 per cent of households having access to any type of toilet facilities (GoI, 2002a: 19). This low coverage rate is despite many years of effort by international donor agencies and NGOs to improve environmental sanitation, and millions of dollars being spent every year. Thousands of latrines have been built with the assistance of government schemes but remain unused and have fallen into disrepair; possible reasons for this are outlined on pp. 22–5. Sanitation is largely missing in the political agenda in India, says WaterAid, and the poor progress in rural sanitation is a major cause of concern (WAI, 2005).

To meet MDG Target 10, almost 51 million people (on average) must gain access to some form of latrine every year of the decade to 2015. For comparison purposes, just over 22 million were served every year (on average) from 1990 to 2004. The official WHO comment is that India is 'making progress but insufficient'.

WAI statistics (shown in Table 2.2) illustrate that 53 per cent of the Indian rural population (438 million people) must have access to some form of latrine by 2015. That is a huge challenge, requiring some 21 million rural people per year (on average) in the period 2000–15 gaining access to and using basic, hygienic, sanitation. For comparison purposes, around 7.5 million rural people per year gained access to a latrine in the period 1990–2000. Progress has been so slow over the last 10 years, say WAI (2005), and coverage remains so poor, that despite huge financial

Table 2.2 Numbers to be served to meet the MDGs in India

	Coverage (% population and million of people served/to be served by 2015)			No. of new people to serve each year
	1990	*2000*	*2015 MDG*	
Rural water	41%	94%?	70.5%	13 million
	260 million		583 million	
Rural sanitation	6%	15%	53%	21 million
	38 million		438 million	

Source: WAI, 2005.

allocations committed under the 10th Five-Year Plan to the rural drinking water sector, it looks unlikely that India will reach the MDG target for rural sanitation unless there is a 'rapid acceleration in progress'.

Even if the MDG targets are met, a huge number of people will still remain uncovered. Almost half the rural population, some 388 million people, will still be without basic sanitation; and 29 per cent, 244 million people, will lack access to safe, sustainable water.

Socio-economic conditions in Orissa

The population of Orissa is close to 38 million, of whom about 87 per cent lives in rural areas. The majority of the population are Hindu-Indians, with about 25 per cent being *adivasi* (indigenous tribal people, designated as Scheduled Tribes, ST, by the GoI) and 17 percent being *dalit* ('oppressed' or 'downtrodden', designated as Scheduled Caste, SC, by the GoI). The official state language is Oriya; *adivasi* have their own languages but they use Oriya to communicate with others. The average income per head in Orissa is US$250, 58 per cent of the national average in 2001–2; 17.5 million people (almost 40 per cent of the population) lives below the national poverty line (BPL) (DFID, 2005).[6] Poverty is significantly worse in the western and southern districts of the state where *adivasi* and *dalit* constitute the majority of the population. Table 2.3 shows some asset-based measures of poverty, comparing Orissa to the whole of India.

Orissa is an eastern state (see Map 2.1) and most people live in rural areas. The state is rich in natural resources and yet it is one of the poorest states of the country. The economic potential of Orissa seems big: it has a lot of minerals and would seem suitable for tourists, having forest, lakes, a long coastline, and a rich and ancient culture and history. However Orissa attracts only a few tourists, maybe because it is too far from the tourist centre of the country near New Delhi. There is some industry, mainly in the north where there are deposits of iron, manganese, coal and mica. In GDP terms, 32 per cent comes from agriculture and 62 per cent of the people work in agriculture (de Wit, 2005).

The state has hardly profited from the Indian economic growth: the percentage of people BPL in Orissa did not decrease significantly between 1994 and 2000, whereas it dropped 20 per cent in the country overall (Mackinnon, 2002). The dismal economic condition has a direct bearing on the living conditions and quality of life of the poor, especially in rural areas. Development of basic infrastructure and access to basic services, essential drivers for social development and economic growth, has only happened in the cities and accessible rural areas. An indicator of this is that in rural Orissa less than 20 per cent have access to protected water, and less than 1 per cent to piped water supply. Less than 5 per cent have access to sanitation.

Table 2.3 Income-based measures of poverty: households having assets, %

Asset	Orissa	India
House	96	95
Kutcha house (mud/thatch)	80	55
Electricity connection	19	43
Protected water	49	72
Piped water	24	25
Tube well	1	9
Toilet	4 (lowest in India)	15
Bicycle	56	54
TV	6	12
Radio	30	38

Source: Mackinnon, 2002 (table 2.1).

In lowland Orissa the economy is mainly based on agriculture, a major crop being paddy rice grown by subsistence farmers. Agriculture is not as developed as in other states, with little irrigation and few modern methods or inputs (Mackinnon, 2002). Large farmers constitute 2 per cent of the farmers, but control 24 per cent of the land; a third of the rural population is landless, owning only the land on which their homestead is built. There is high seasonal unemployment: year after year when the planting and harvesting seasons are over a large section of the poor migrate in search of work in order to avoid starvation.

The region is subject to frequent natural disasters. In 90 of the last 100 years it has been afflicted by droughts, floods and cyclones. These disasters seriously affect the poor, with their houses of mud and dependence on rain-fed agriculture.

Within Orissa there are large economic differences: the inland regions are in general poorer than the coastal, the rural areas are poorer than the urban areas and the tribal villages are poorer than the General Caste (GC) villages. Also, within GC villages there are differences, with lower-caste people mostly among the poorest. With most development reaching the better-off people in the cities, these differences are widening. Orissa has extensive forested hills inland from the narrow coastal plain and many *adivasi* groups live in inaccessible villages in these hills. They derive their livelihoods largely from the forests, woodcutting being a major source of income (Mackinnon, 2002). *Adivasi* are technically outside the caste system, but most Hindu-Indians consider them lower (see Appendix 1 for a brief synopsis of the caste system). *Adivasi* are generally treated very poorly, suffering exploitation by moneylenders, dispossession and widespread hunger. There are many government schemes to help *adivasi*, but the people do not know their entitlements and corruption is rife.

Orissa is a very conservative state, in a conservative country, and it is generally considered that a female's place is in the home (see Appendix 2

Map 2.1 Location of Orissa in India
Source: www.mapsofindia.com

for an outline of rural women's autonomy). In many villages women will not leave the house except to carry out essential tasks like fetch water or firewood, and even then they will cover their faces entirely with their sari. Table 2.4 shows the level of literacy in Orissa and India: almost two-thirds of the national and state population are literate, but only just over half the female population of Orissa is literate. MacKinnon found (2002) the general picture in Orissa to be that more boys than girls are enrolled in primary schools, but there are markedly fewer children in higher grades. For instance there were 169,000 children in grade 5 in 2001 compared with 315,000 in grade 1; this would seem to indicate a high drop-out rate from school.

Table 2.4 Level of literacy in Orissa and India, %

	Orissa	India
Male	76	76
Female	51	54
Total population	64	65

Source: Mackinnon, 2002 (table 2.3), figures from 2001 census.

Water, sanitation and health

Mackinnon found (2002) that in Orissa only 49 per cent of people have protected water and only 4 per cent have a toilet, which is the lowest number in India. Most people who have these facilities live in the cities. The coverage in rural Orissa is much worse (see Table 2.5); the World Bank (2003) found that less than 20 per cent has access to protected water (less than 1 per cent to piped water supply) and less than 5 per cent has access to some form of a latrine. Villagers mostly do not take initiatives themselves to agitate for basic services as they are often divided along economic, caste and tribe lines (see Box 2.1 for an example).

For centuries the people of Orissa have practised open defecation. In many parts of Orissa, and indeed the Indian subcontinent, it is common to see men defecating on the roadsides or in the fields, usually in the mornings or evenings. At daybreak and after dark car headlights will pick out startled women in small groups squatting by the roadside, hiding their faces in shame. Also, people defecating outside at night live in fear of snakes and scorpions. With the increasing population,

---

Box 2.1 Apathy in Sana Laupur

Sana Laupur, a village with 29 Saura (tribal) families, posed Gram Vikas a challenge with respect to motivating women to organize themselves. Two savings groups exist in the village, a new and an older one. The new group responded well to Gram Vikas's efforts and boasted of considerable success; but the older group had many defaulters and members refused to attend meetings. They spent their profit and other limited income on liquor and there was a marked apathy towards the efforts of Gram Vikas to motivate them. These women agreed that their greatest enemy was liquor addiction, found even among women. However, they would not come up with a solution but kept lamenting their helplessness and at the slightest sign of any protest by the women, even a meeting, they were subjected to physical abuse at home. Their loans were often misused by their husbands, making repayment difficult. Some felt they could fight the problem with outside help, but most maintained a sceptical silence.

The difference in attitude between the two women's groups to Gram Vikas's assistance was a manifestation of the economic divide in the village. Out of 29 families about 5 are relatively well-off, have their own lands to cultivate and have managed to restrict liquor addiction. These women are members of the newer savings group. The remaining families live in great poverty and are landless, the members of the older group. After much motivation work, the RHEP has now been successfully implemented in Sana Laupur.

many wastelands and small woodlands that were previously used for defecating are now fenced off for farming or construction. This is why the women are driven to this twice-daily round of humiliation on the sides of the roads, which have effectively become open-air toilets for the majority of the population. Even roads in town are not exempt from this kind of use. After a heavy shower of rain in the slummy and crowded areas of Berhampur town, people are forced to wade through a filthy mess composed of mud, rubbish and human excreta.

Mackinnon found (2002: 5) that 62 per cent of ill-health in Orissa was due to communicable diseases (see Table 2.6), and that this figure was higher than for the rest of India. Unfortunately Mackinnon does not explain exactly what is included in his term 'communicable diseases'. Rural people generally bathe and wash their clothes in the village pond or river, water which is polluted by the open-defecation practice and wallowing animals. Women are forced to bathe fully clothed to preserve their dignity (see Plate 2.1). Gram Vikas found that the women in rural Orissa suffered especially from the lack of clean water and proper sanitation facilities: 60 per cent of women had gynaecological problems

Photo 2.1 The multiple uses of a water source in Orissa
Source: Gram Vikas.

Table **2.5** Access to water, sanitation and electricity in rural Orissa, %

Access to:	Protected water	Piped water	Sanitation	Electricity
% of population	<20	<1	<5	~22.6

Source: World Bank (2003).

Table **2.6** Source of ill-health in Orissa and India, %

	Orissa	India
Communicable diseases	62	51
Non-communicable diseases	22	40
Injuries	16	9

Source: Mackinnon, 2002 (table 2.2).

because they could not wash themselves properly when there was no privacy. The practice of having to wait until dark to relieve themselves, to avoid the shame and embarrassment of being seen, is also a contributing factor to gynaecological problems.

Central government's rural water supply strategy

The GoI's Ministry of Rural Development is responsible for rural water supply countrywide. In 1972–3 the GoI introduced the Accelerated Rural Water Supply Programme (ARWSP) to assist the states in increasing the coverage of drinking water supply in rural areas. India has around 1.4 million rural habitations, and up to 2003 the ARWSP provided 29,000 uncovered and 188,000 partially covered habitations with drinking water supply (DDWS, undated). Up until the late 1990s the ARWSP supplied water free of charge to villagers, generally via a handpump or standpipe, and all operation and maintenance (O&M) costs remained the government's responsibility. One drawback was that villagers had no input in the planning or installation of the facility, and no say about how deep the tube well should be: the contractor appeared, drilled the hole and installed the pump, and left without testing the yield. As a result the village handpump or standpipe may not be accessible to all households (e.g. for caste reasons; see Appendix 1 for a brief explanation of the caste system), or the tube well may not be deep enough to produce water in the drier months. Another drawback is that people have no sense of ownership over the facilities, and are not educated in how to use the pump or tap, so breakages are common; because maintenance is a government responsibility it may be a considerable time before the facility is repaired. In the meantime villagers must resort to their previous source of water, which is almost certainly contaminated. So although many villages are deemed by the government to be covered with improved drinking water supply, in effect they are not.

From the start of their RHEP Gram Vikas has insisted that villagers are involved at all stages in planning, construction and O&M of their water supply, realizing that this is vital to generate a sense of ownership over assets and ensure long-term sustainability of the system.

In 1999 the GoI made reforms to the ARWSP on a pilot basis and founded the Department of Drinking Water Supply (DDWS). The programme became demand-driven – the GoI guaranteed to provide a water supply system for any village that asked for one – and the government switched from service provider to a facilitator's role (DDWS, undated). The aim is that villagers are empowered through full participation in the project: from planning, design and implementation, to control of finances, managing the scheme and full ownership of the assets through their village water and sanitation committee; women are to be actively involved. The proportion of capital cost paid by the government depends on the level of service demanded by the village, but the community provides a minimum of 10 per cent of the capital cost either in cash or in kind (labour, materials, land) and is fully responsible for O&M of the resulting water supply. The programme now also encourages conservation measures like rainwater harvesting and groundwater recharge systems. In December 2002 this pilot was scaled up to the whole country as the *Swajaldhara* (availability of good-quality water) scheme.

There are still some shortcomings to the ARWSP. A big drawback is that the *Swajaldhara* scheme remains wide-open to abuse: the planning and construction work is contracted out and, because they make such large profits, the contractors have no problem in contributing the 10 per cent of cost that the villagers are supposed to pay. So, in effect, many villages get their water system free. Problems then arise when it comes to O&M costs because people feel no ownership, and because they have not had to unite to get the water system installed they feel no sense of community spirit to collectively look after their asset, so it all slowly falls apart.

Another drawback is that the GoI only undertakes to provide 40 litres water per person per day and there is no provision for water storage (or, if villagers insist on storage, storage of 10 litres per adult is the maximum that the government will fund). Power shortages mean that water can only be pumped at restricted times, so, without storage, villages still have no water for most of the day – running water is considered a luxury that the rural masses do not need. Gram Vikas helps villages to avail themselves of government funds through the *Swajaldhara* scheme, but here the infrastructure is upgraded to allow for 35 litres water storage per person and taps in all households, so that running water is available all day.

The *Swajaldhara* scheme is implemented through the *panchayat raj* institutions (PRIs) in each state (see Box 2.2 for an introduction to the

PRIs). Central government disburses *Swajaldhara* funds to the state government, from there it goes to the District Drinking Water and Sanitation Missions and from there to the village water and sanitation committees.

In Orissa, the state government's Ministry of Rural Development implements the ARWSP through their Minimum Need Programme. The programme is implemented in each district by its District Water and Sanitation Mission, but the Department of Rural Development says that the overall efficiency of the programme needs to be improved by establishing inter-sector linkages. The state claimed to have achieved coverage of more than 99 per cent of the population, but ran into

---

Box 2.2 The *panchayat raj* institution (PRI), the local government system in India

India is a federal republic divided into 28 states and 7 union territories. States are usually sub-divided into 20–30 districts each comprising approximately 50 blocks, and each block comprises approximately 50 villages. The structure of the PRI was laid down in a constitutional amendment in 1993. It consists of a three-tier system of democratically elected local governments, namely the district *panchayat*, the block *panchayat* and the *gram panchayat* (village council, GP) – see diagram.

A GP covers a population of more than 500, so it may cover more than one habitation. The GP comprises ward members representing different parts of the GP. Members of the GP are elected directly by the village's registered voters, and some seats are reserved for women (33%), SC and ST. The elected members of the GP elect from among themselves a *sarpanch* (leader of the GP). Drinking water and sanitation are only one of the GP's many areas of responsibility. Funding for water and sanitation comes from the state government, through the districts and blocks to the GPs.

Local elections are now held throughout India and the *panchayats* have the potential for a degree of self-government – the *sarpanch* has become an important local figure – but the real strength of the GP lies in lobbying block and district officials.

Sources: Gunyon (1998: 6); Wiki (undated).

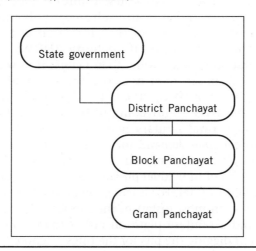

difficulties with unsustainable sources and problems with water quality. The programme aims to provide a safe water source for every 5–10 households, through either a standpipe or a handpump; however, maintenance and repair is often lacking, so facilities fail. Queues of people at working taps and pumps are a common sight. Many villages in Orissa effectively still rely on the village pond for drinking water and washing.

Central government's strategy for sanitation

In India sanitation was not historically perceived as a priority by the government, especially in rural areas where open space was readily available. The first initiative for rural sanitation, the Central Rural Sanitation Programme (CRSP), was introduced in 1986 following increased population growth and urbanization. The objective of the programme was to improve the quality of life of rural people and provide privacy for women, restoring their dignity. The CRSP provided a 100 per cent subsidy for construction of sanitary latrines; the subsidy's allocation was primarily based on poverty criteria. The programme was supply driven, did not motivate recipients or allow for their participation in decision-making, and emphasized a single latrine design (pour-flush toilets) that proved expensive. As a result, even if toilet facilities were created they were found in many cases not to be used. Of the sanitary pour flush toilets constructed in the 1980s and 1990s, less than 50 per cent were found in use (DDWS, undated).

This high-subsidy approach of the CRSP was revised by the GoI in 1999, when the Total Sanitation Campaign (TSC) was introduced as a countrywide strategy for improving the performance of rural sanitation. The main sanitation goal of the GoI is to eradicate the practice of open defecation by 2010. The TSC advocates 'a shift from a high subsidy to a low subsidy regime, greater household involvement, demand responsiveness, and providing for the promotion of a range of toilet options to promote increased affordability' (DDWS, undated). The concept of sanitation is much wider than before: it now includes liquid and solid waste disposal, food hygiene, and personal, domestic and environmental hygiene (WAI, 2005). The TSC principles are people-centred, demand-driven and community-led, emphasizing social marketing through rural sanitary marts and production centres; and IEC in order to generate demand for sanitation facilities.

Under the TSC a subsidy is given as an incentive to BPL households for the construction of individual pit latrines, but only for toilets costing less than INR2,000 in total. For a INR2,000 latrine the government will provide INR1,200.[7] In most instances the subsidy takes the form of four cement rings and a sanitary platform rather than cash, which means that, if the cost of digging the pits for the rings is ignored, the household may only spend INR800 in building the superstructure. Gram Vikas says that the TSC assumes that the concerned household will construct the superstructure for their toilet at their own cost if they are merely 'enlightened' regarding the need for sanitation, that continuous motivation is not necessary. As a result only 5–10 per cent of households bother to build the superstructure. The vast majority of government toilets end up with partially-completed walls, so that there is no privacy and most toilets have never been used (see Photo 2.2). There are countless cases where the cement platform of the toilet is being used as a washing platform, after filling up the hole in the middle.

The lack of running water in the TSC's subsidized toilets is cited by Gram Vikas as another reason for many latrines being unused, since the norm in India is to use water for anal cleansing. Gram Vikas says: 'The toilet is built close to the house; if it is not cleaned it stinks, and nobody wants a stink close to their house so they choose not to use the toilet. Why would someone who is comfortable with open defecation walk 1 km to fetch water [for cleaning the toilet and for anal cleansing]? Who would be agreeable to using such ill-designed toilets?' Although

Photo 2.2 Typical example of a toilet built under the government's TSC
Source: Gram Vikas.

the TSC only gives subsidies for low-cost pit latrines, one of its main objectives is 'to convert all dry latrines into sanitary pour-flush latrines'. The hope is that BPL households will gradually upgrade to construct a better facility at their own cost (DDWS, undated).

Other problems with the TSC mentioned by Gram Vikas are that households that are not BPL are not targeted for sanitation and will continue to defecate in the open, probably close to a water source, so faecal-oral disease will persist. As with every government program there is a lot of corruption. The government's definition of BPL is too simple and the few villages that profit are often the better-off ones with better access to government officials. The result is that not always the poorest people are helped.

In 2003 the GoI announced the *Nirmal Gram Puraskar* (Clean Village Award), a cash incentive scheme for GPs, blocks and districts that are fully sanitized and free of open defecation; rewards range from INR10,000 to INR500,000. The amount of money received is based on population criteria and depends on 100 per cent sanitation coverage of individual households and of schools, freedom from open defecation and maintenance of a clean environment.

In 2004–5 the GoI introduced a school sanitation scheme to the TSC, to encourage wider acceptance of sanitation by children. Under this scheme INR20,000 is given to each school to build toilets for girls and boys. Again no water is provided, and no hygiene education is given, so people do not understand the reason for using the toilets or the need to clean them or wash their hands with soap, so the toilets rapidly fall into disuse and people are back to open defecation and girls stop going to school.

The TSC is being implemented in 426 districts of the country with funding support from the GoI, the relevant state governments and communities. The GoI has reported rapid growth in coverage levels since 1998 as a result of the TSC (WAI, 2006). Of the almost 140 million rural households in India nearly 4.4 million have constructed household toilets under the TSC. Likewise, over 1,750 women's complexes, 41,854 school toilets, 5,238 *anganwadi* (crèche) toilets, and 618 production centres/rural sanitary marts have been set up.

Gram Vikas believes that the TSC will probably work well enough in regions where there is some tradition of fixed-point defecation, such as Kerala, parts of West Bengal and Gujarat. But where open defecation has been the rule for centuries it expects it will take a lot more than cement rings and a squat pad to bring about a change in people's habits and practices. For this reason Gram Vikas says that in states like Orissa, Uttar Pradesh, undivided Bihar and undivided Madhya Pradesh the GoI's TSC scheme has been 'a tremendous drain on public money and absolutely no sanitation has taken place'.

Box 2.3 Maharashtra state's community-led TSC – a success story

Each state in India has its own interpretation of how to implement the central government's TSC. Most states are still using a supply-driven approach despite the fact that the GoI state that the TSC 'is not a target oriented or a supply driven program'. The Government of Maharashtra (GoM) is a clear exception since it has adopted a community-led total sanitation approach, shifting from the old policy of targeting households with individual construction subsidies to targeting the community with community rewards (MahaWSSD, undated). The campaign is supplemented by two cash-incentive based schemes: the *Nirmal Gram Puraskar* (explained on p. 24) and the Clean Village Campaign (CVC). The CVC offers annual cash prizes to clean villages with the aim of educating and motivating rural communities.

Another important aspect of the GoM's revised approach is that they only release the TSC subsidy to BPL households once the entire GP is free of open defecation. This incentive has spurred villagers and *panchayat* officials to explore innovative methods to achieve total sanitation in their villages. The campaign is no longer supply-driven and target-oriented, it is driven by community demand. The state government has made remarkable progress in having more than 1,600 GPs in the state achieve an open-defecation-free status.

Sanitation does not earn votes, and most of the Indian population do not see the need for sanitation – they have been practising open defecation for centuries and have little desire to change. To overcome this indifference it is necessary to motivate people and create a demand for sanitation. GoI now realizes that throwing money at the problem will not in itself solve it, that a vigorous IEC campaign is needed. However, maintaining the momentum of an IEC campaign is difficult; IEC will always suffer when infrastructural targets have to be met. A study in Andhra Pradesh showed IEC to be the missing link in rural sanitation (GoI, 2005). The study found that some villagers flatly refused to construct individual sanitary toilets on the grounds that the house is meant for eating in and it must be clean. Those who had constructed toilets were not using them due to the foul smell, a fear of mosquitoes or lack of cleaning facilities for the soak pits when it gets filled. An assessment of Gram Vikas's work in Samiapalli by SDC (2000) showed that women had overcome this taboo on sanitation by using detergents to keep the toilets clean.

According to WAI (2005), the state and district level Water and Sanitation Missions are ill-staffed and ineffective. There is not enough political decentralization, so that PRIs have a limited role of implementation. There is a lack of long-term planning at the levels of district and block: the role of NGOs and civil society is inadequately defined, and a lack of prioritization and funding for O&M leads to disrepair of water sources. In a different study (WAI, 2006), WAI says that the 'plethora' of government schemes tend to work in contradiction. The two major GoI programmes, *Swajaldhara* and TSC, do not explicitly make a connection between the water supply and sanitation. Water and sanitation, though spoken about together in debates, are not promoted together in practice. This is a serious flaw, since the improper disposal of wastes leads to continued contamination of water bodies. The schemes need better convergence: in the absence of a holistic approach, WAI (2006) say, total sanitation will not easily be achieved.

The role of partner organizations in extending coverage

CSOs have been long-time critics of governments for 'failing to meet their responsibility of ensuring universal basic water and sanitation rights of their people' (ADB, 2006: 3). For many years they have been advocating for changes in policy and greater allocation of resources to water supply and sanitation, recognizing this as an important entry-point for poverty alleviation. As a result of this advocacy many governments have given rural water supply and sanitation a higher priority, says the ADB. These governments have also come to realize that they cannot do the job alone, and now take advantage of the knowledge, skills and resources (technical and financial) that other partners with many years of experience can bring to water supply and sanitation projects.

Civil society-led initiatives, says the ADB (2006), are usually community-based, aimed to improve the lives of the poor, in places which are not considered by private-service providers to be profitable to invest in. Interventions tend to focus more on capacity-building of both the communities, which are expected to manage the systems, and the government. The government's role is slowly evolving from being a service provider to being a facilitator and supporter of the community management systems.

Some CSOs act as support networks to other CSOs which in turn do the direct grassroots work. This type of support network helps to share knowledge and build capacities among members through the dissemination of lessons learned by other members, the result being that more areas can be reached and sustainability is increased. These networks 'also have a stronger collective voice in advocacy work ... [and their] understanding of the realities on the ground put them into a central [position in discussions]' (ADB, 2006: 5)

Many donors are now recognizing the value of working through a partnership between CSOs and governments, as evidenced from the amount of resources channelled directly through CSOs (ADB, 2006: 5). Working in collaboration with CSO partners can help to bridge the service delivery gap by increasing coverage and sustainability of water and sanitation services for the rural poor.

CHAPTER 3
Introducing Gram Vikas

This chapter introduces Gram Vikas: its background, its vision for the rural poor, its core values and its programme interventions. The ethos behind the RHEP is explored, as are its key elements.

What is Gram Vikas?

Gram Vikas, a non-partisan secular voluntary NGO, works with poor and marginalized communities in Orissa.[8]

Gram Vikas's vision is: 'An equitable and sustainable society where people live in peace with dignity'. Their mission is: 'To promote processes which are sustainable, socially inclusive and gender equitable, to enable

---

Box 3.1 Gram Vikas's core values

All of Gram Vikas's work is governed by five core values: social equity, inclusion, gender equity, cost-sharing and sustainability.

Social equity: poor people should not have to suffer poor-quality solutions, and every member of a community should have access to the same facilities and opportunities. Government has put much more effort into urban than rural development, severely neglecting and further marginalizing remote areas; Gram Vikas aims to empower united rural communities to claim from the government their right to the same level of services they could expect in a city; their goal is to reduce rural-to-urban migration.

Inclusion: the exclusion of the marginalized over the centuries (by the state, the markets, their fellow-villagers and, more recently, some development agencies) has instilled in them the belief that it is their fate and they deserve no better. Gram Vikas – via its 100 per cent policy, that is, the participation of all households – includes marginalized groups so as to raise their self-esteem, awareness and capacity.

Gender equity: it is Gram Vikas's goal to overcome gender inequality by promoting equal rights to service, opportunity and participation for both men and women, and by empowering women to come together and become economically independent from their husbands or fathers.

Cost-sharing: development work should not be charity, which creates dependence and strengthens the feeling among poor communities of being unable to change their situation. Gram Vikas believes that all stakeholders (donors, the state, project beneficiaries) should contribute to community development: even the poorest should pay in cash, labour or materials, thus gaining self-respect and a sense of ownership. Gram Vikas tries to ensure an equitable division of costs, with better-off families cross-subsidizing poorer families.

Sustainability: in order for project benefits to endure even after Gram Vikas's withdrawal it is vital to build the capacity of communities to manage, finance and operate their facilities so that there is 100 per cent coverage at all times.

critical masses of poor and marginalized rural people or communities to achieve a dignified quality of life'.

Gram Vikas works through a range of programmes with project teams of 12–15 staff members, supported by volunteers in the villages.[9] As at 31 March 2007 the NGO served a population of over 187,000 (around 36,000 households) across 550 villages throughout Orissa.

The NGO's interventions are directed at raising critical consciousness and energizing whole villages. They aim to reduce the vulnerability of isolated and impoverished communities by improving people's living conditions and livelihood options. This will enable communities to gradually 'emerge from the vicious cycle of poverty to a spiral of sustained growth' (Gram Vikas, 2007) where they have the confidence to take charge of their own development.

The NGO was founded in 1979 by a small group of student volunteers who had originally come from Madras (Chennai) in 1971, with the Young Students' Movement for Development (YSMD), to set up relief camps and return and resettle people affected by the war for independence in Bangladesh. When a cyclone caused a huge tidal wave to hit coastal Orissa in October 1971, rendering over 1 million people homeless, 40 of the original YSMD group rushed to Orissa to help people in the relief and rehabilitation. During that time the volunteers became acutely aware of the poverty and underdevelopment of the people. 'There were no NGOs or other development agencies, except for some missionary backward areas.' (Gram Vikas, 2007) The volunteers first tried to help people with their agricultural practices, their main source of livelihood; but they found that all their hard work only resulted in more income for the landed class. This led them to rethink their strategies and work towards social equity.

An opportunity presented itself when the District Collector of Ganjam invited the group to initiate a dairy cooperative for the *adivasi* of the Kerandimal region. The Berhampur Milk Producers' Co-Operative offered land in Mohuda, in the foothills of Kerandimal, and the group started working from there in 1976. It did not take them long to realize that dairying was not feasible: there was no infrastructure or veterinary support, and, more significantly, the tribal people believed that cow's milk was not meant for human consumption. They also saw that the people had more urgent needs. 'We started talking to people, especially women, trying to gain their confidence and understand their needs. The first thing to strike us was the abysmal health conditions in the villages – malaria was rampant. No one understood the relevance of safe drinking water, healthy food or hygiene. And of course there were no dispensaries or clinics within accessible distances.' (Gram Vikas, 2007) The group put in place a rudimentary health-care service in the villages, and started an intensive programme for training village health workers. This initial strategy of using health as the entry point was good in terms of creating goodwill. Slowly, the people began to trust the group and discuss their problems.

The tribal people had a strong distrust of outsiders, justifiably so because the outsiders they knew were only interested in occupying their land and denying them access to the meagre resources they had. Most of them had no land; if they did it was mortgaged to moneylenders. All of them were bonded labourers. The liquor merchants made sure that they spent what little they had on drink, which made them further indebted; they had no way of paying back the money they owed. They were aware of the injustice but had no way of protesting. In 1978 the Indian government declared a moratorium on rural indebtedness. This policy provided the legal support to launch a campaign to mobilize the tribal people around the issue of land mortgaging. In what came to be known as 'people's courts', the tribal people arbitrated every case of mortgaging in the presence of moneylenders. This was accompanied by a social boycott of the exploitative people and organized demonstrations at the district headquarters. By the end of 1979, nearly every case in the Kerandimal region had been settled in favour of the tribal people. The tribals had tasted victory for the first time.

'By the end of 1978, we began to realize that we had very little in common with the YSMD back in Madras. Living in a remote village, witnessing the perils of relentless poverty and indebtedness had given us a perspective that was essentially different from any theoretical awareness. Support from those who remained with the mainstream was negligible. It was time to set up a new organization.' (Gram Vikas, 2007) Gram Vikas was born on 22 January 1979 and registered under the Societies Registration Act 1860.

The 1980s saw Gram Vikas working in two distinct approaches to development, both concerned with improving the quality of life of the poor. The Integrated Tribal Development Programme (ITDP) was based on awareness generation, the organization of communities and delivery of education and health services, with a view to developing the capacities of the *adivasi* communities, because in these remote and inaccessible habitations there is an acute shortage of even the most basic government services. This spread to other sectors including the protection and regeneration of natural resources and the development of livelihoods and infrastructure. The goal of the ITDP is to help the tribal people move towards a more secure lifestyle and become self-reliant and adapt to the changing conditions of their environment. The programme has developed over the years from being welfare-driven and service-oriented to recognizing that people's participation and ownership are essential for sustainable community development.

The second development approach in the 1980s was the promotion of biogas as a cheap alternative means of energy to firewood. Biogas was being heavily promoted by the GoI through the National Biogas

Development Programme. Gram Vikas's thrust was large-scale dissemination of the technology with built-in mechanisms for maintenance, repairs and further expansion. Between 1983 and 1993, Gram Vikas built 80 per cent (about 55,000 plants) of all biogas plants constructed in Orissa during that period. Perhaps more important than the number of plants was the associated upgrading of people's skills in the process: creating a body of trained masons (over 6,000), technicians and supervisors (over 600). While the ITDP was confined to remote tribal areas of Ganjam, Gajapati and Kalahandi districts of Orissa, through the biogas programme Gram Vikas worked with a wide cross-section of poor communities across the length and breadth of Orissa. From 1994 Gram Vikas started the process of spinning off the biogas programme, encouraging the supervisors and masons to set up on their own, or with other local voluntary organizations, to promote biogas, with Gram Vikas's technical support and backing for bank loans. In 1997 Gram Vikas conducted a survey of the biogas plants that they had constructed: 82 per cent were still in operation.

Gram Vikas's two decades of development experience had taught it that all too often development schemes address people selectively: the people who can make use of schemes are often those who are economically stronger, and when they draw exclusive benefit from a scheme it effectively widens the economic divide within the community. What is worse is that it reinforces the belief of the poorest of the poor that they are not equal citizens and are not worth caring about, adding to their very low self-esteem. Gram Vikas aimed to overcome these ingrained attitudes by getting all households in a village involved in any further development programme. Gram Vikas's experience to date had been that once a threshold quality of life is reached people start to realize their power and believe in their abilities; this can trigger a spiralling development process.

Origins and aim of Gram Vikas's water and sanitation work

Through the biogas programme Gram Vikas had worked with many poor non-tribal communities across the state. It realized that it had established a trust among the villagers, that it delivered on what it promised, whereas the government was perceived by and large as not being able to deliver. Gram Vikas felt that it should build on this goodwill to address other aspects of peoples' lives. It saw the need for integrated development strategies to address the low quality of life of the poor: chronic poverty, limited livelihood opportunities, underdevelopment and a general apathy. When Gram Vikas asked villagers what they needed most, they identified a hospital as a need because they were constantly falling ill, suffering from diarrhoea, malaria, jaundice and other waterborne diseases. Their water sources were unprotected, contaminated by human and animal faecal matter.

Gram Vikas saw that all households in these villages were affected by poor health due to unsanitary practices. Water- and sanitation-related ailments are one of the main causes of ill-health and low economic standards in rural areas of Orissa. So water and sanitation became the entry-point for Gram Vikas's new development programme, the RHEP, which was started in 1992. Sanitation and water is just a step towards a larger goal of energizing communities and enabling them to start their own development, to lift them out of feeling that it is their fate to be destitute and there is nothing they can do about it. The core thrust of the RHEP is to harness the physical, natural, social and human capital in every village through convergent community action, to create a spiralling process of development. Through the RHEP intervention Gram Vikas creates unity in the village, fosters leadership among the people and addresses gender inequity in order to create an environment for the people to take up the initiative for development work which they themselves decide upon, direct and manage. In its evolution the programme has drawn on the strengths of, and lessons learned from, the ITDP and biogas programmes.

The hardware constructed consists of toilets and bathing rooms for every family in the village, and running water supply to three taps in all houses (kitchen, toilet, bathing room) via a water tank. But the RHEP places equal emphasis on the 'software' of development: community contribution and management, skill-building, education. Financial and institutional mechanisms are created to ensure that these services and facilities are available to all families in the village without exception, even in the future. All households are included, and all female heads of household are involved in decision-making.

A process of total village development based on building toilets before the water supply (the reason for this is explained on p. 46) was a difficult concept for anyone to accept initially. Many of Gram Vikas's staff were disbelieving, the communities approached had their reservations and no donor agency would believe in it. Gram Vikas started in a small way in five pilot villages covering 337 families, building on the contacts established during the biogas programme. In 1998 the programme was expanded to include 35 more villages covering 3,078 families; by 31 March 2007 a total of almost 27,000 families were covered.

The RHEP's primary focus is on *adivasi, dalit* and other poor and marginalized sections, like the landless and small or marginal farmers. In most villages covered by the project, more than 80 per cent of the families are BPL. The focus of Gram Vikas's work in terms of geographical coverage is on districts in the hinterlands across the south and southwest and in remote parts of the north. The RHEP process has also been implemented in some ITDP villages. Gram Vikas works through its project offices across the state; the majority of staff are drawn from the local area.

Since 2004 Gram Vikas's strategic orientation has been towards an integrated habitat development programme, integrating the ITDP and the RHEP approaches under the umbrella of the Movement and Action Network for Transformation of Rural Areas (MANTRA). MANTRA facilitates united and capacitated communities to undertake development activities in the following focal areas: enabling infrastructure, self-governing people's institutions, health, education, livelihoods and food security. Gram Vikas's responses are context-specific based on the needs and priorities of the community involved, since given the diverse social and economic contexts in villages the importance of the MANTRA focal areas varies. Gram Vikas's MANTRA vision is represented visually in Photo 3.1.

Gram Vikas has received much recognition for its work, including the World Hunger Award from Brown University, the Tech Laureate from Tech Museum and multiple national awards. Joe Madiath (Executive Director of Gram Vikas) was nominated for the Social Lifetime Achievement Award 2005 from the Red & White Bravery Awards. The citation read:

Photo 3.1 Gram Vikas's MANTRA vision
Source: Gram Vikas.

We are happy to inform you that you have been nominated to receive the Social Lifetime Achievement Award for Social Service for your contribution in improving the plight of the rural masses, by expanding the economic options available to them and in restoring dignity to marginalized populations. Your work with Gram Vikas, of harnessing through full community mobilization, all physical and human capital in a village, has been outstanding.

Gram Vikas has received the following international accolades specifically for its water and sanitation-based development programme:

- Most Innovative Development Project 2001 by the Global Development Network, an institution established by the World Bank for promoting research and innovations in development.
- World Habitat Award from UN Habitat in 2003.
- Kyoto World Water Grand Prize in 2006 (the first time this prize was awarded). Gram Vikas was one of 30 finalists selected from over 450 entries of local action projects from all across the globe. The prize was awarded at the fourth World Water Forum, an initiative of the World Water Council, which is an international organization based in Marseilles, France. In awarding the prize, the Forum acknowledged the 'excellent contribution [of Gram Vikas] to building dignity through community-managed rural water and sanitation, thus improving the livelihoods of the poor and marginalized in Orissa, one of the poorest states of India'.
- Joint winner of two Ashoka Changemakers Innovation Award Competitions in 2006: How to improve health for all and How to improve housing for all.
- The India NGO Award, 2006 for promoting transparency, accountability and good governance. The award was given by the Nand and Jeet Khemka Foundation, India in collaboration with Resource Alliance, UK. The Nand and Jeet Khemka Foundation is an independent foundation with a mission to develop and promote institutions that make a substantial impact on poverty, deprivation and the degradation of human and natural environment.
- Skoll Award for Social Entrepreneurship 2007. The Skoll Foundation was created by eBay's first president, Jeff Skoll, to promote his vision of a more peaceful and prosperous world. The foundation invests in social entrepreneurs.

Rural development's social costs

Gram Vikas feels that, although rural people can and will pay for services that they want, they have a right to services that fulfil their basic needs. 'To put the issue in perspective, it is only the rural people who are forced to pay for investment in essential services – often by taking loans. In cities, water supply systems, infrastructure, electricity, street lighting, sewerage, drainage, education and health are all heavily subsidized by the state.' (Gram Vikas, 2006a)

This brings Gram Vikas to the conclusion that there are social costs involved in making basic services available to the disadvantaged which governments and general society must bear. Gram Vikas draws upon a large network of government, donor and private-sector resources to assist with these social costs. In support of Gram Vikas's argument it should be noted that complete water and sanitation coverage was not achieved for much of western Europe, the US and Canada until there was massive expenditure by governments between the 1880s and 1950s (Cardone and Fonseca, 2006).

Gram Vikas provides a subsidy of INR3,000 per family for construction of toilets and bathing rooms; this is considered as the social cost. On top of that BPL households get the GoI's TSC subsidy (described on p. 22). Gram Vikas's subsidy is typically given in the form of externally sourced materials: toilet pan, door, cement and steel for roof casting.[10] To meet the cost of the water supply, Gram Vikas helps the villagers to access funds from the government's *Swajaldhara* programme (described on p. 20).

Key elements of Gram Vikas's approach to rural sanitation

All or none, in-built financial sustainability, paying for use, taking responsibility and participatory management are the key elements of the RHEP's approach. Before any intervention in water supply and sanitation can happen there are some non-negotiable rules that must be agreed to by all community heads of household, male and female, as follows.

- Every male and female head of household has to agree to join the programme, ensuring participation by the whole community; this is the all-or- none aspect, 100 percent consensus.
- The water supply will not be connected until all households have a latrine; water is the carrot used to stop open defecation.
- Each family is required to contribute INR1,000, on average, to a community corpus fund, which is held in a deposit account and will fund future expansion of the programme to new families so that no family in the village will ever be without a toilet and bathing room. (How this fund is used is explained further below.)

These rules are based on the premise that in order to eliminate water- and sanitation-related diseases it is vital to totally end the practice of open defecation: even one family left out would mean that diseases would still be transmitted through polluted water or unsanitary habits. Involving all male and female heads of household, including the marginalized, is the first step in breaking down caste and gender barriers and raising the self-esteem of the marginalized.

In-built financial sustainability

Gram Vikas places a heavy emphasis on community contribution. It insists that even the poorest communities come together and use their ingenuity to meet more than 50 per cent of the capital costs of toilets and bathing rooms and 30 per cent of the capital cost of water supply, and also find ways of covering O&M costs. As well as the upfront corpus fund contribution, each household agrees to contribute to the costs of construction – either in money or in kind – and to pay a monthly fee for the O&M costs of the water supply.

The corpus fund ensures that in the future all households will have a sanitation and water supply. When new households set up in the village after the RHEP has been implemented, the interest from the corpus fund will be used to provide a subsidy for external materials so that they can construct a toilet and bathing room (just as Gram Vikas provides a subsidy for these materials to all existing households when the RHEP is being implemented). Thus, the responsibility of meeting the social costs, described above, is taken over by the village. Generating this fund also creates a sense of pride and ownership among the villagers for what they have achieved and the assets they have built. The interest on the corpus fund can also be used to increase the capacity of the water tank, or for any other major infrastructural capital expenses. The capital in the corpus fund cannot, under any circumstances, be touched.

Payments to the corpus fund are calculated in an equitable manner by the village general body (made up of all male and female heads of household), which decides how much each household will pay. Usually the better-off families cross-subsidize the poorer by paying more than INR1,000, and the poorer pay less, but even the poorest household gives at least INR100. Exactly how villagers come up with the corpus fund money is described on pp. 98–100.

Self-management

The water and sanitation programme provides an opportunity for the community to manage resources through village committees. Gram Vikas slips into the role of trainer and, later on, facilitator, building the capacity of the villagers to run their own affairs so that Gram Vikas can withdraw from the village in a phased manner upon completion of the programme. This prevents creating dependency on an external agency. After the implementation of the water and sanitation project Gram Vikas accompanies the people for a period of between three and five years, in capacity-building and establishing gender and social equity.

Good-quality water and sanitation facilities

'The notion that rural masses basically need only low-cost (taken to mean low-quality) solutions to their problems is by now a part of the [bureaucratic] psyche ... A history of short-term low-quality fixes to their problems has contributed to rural people's low self-esteem' (Gram Vikas, 2006a). The cheapest solution to the problem of low coverage in rural water and sanitation may not be the cheapest in the long run. Good-quality service infrastructure is essential to restore dignity to communities; low-quality and soon to be dysfunctional solutions hinder rather than help in achieving sanitation. Through its early experiences, Gram Vikas realized that unless one can provide toilets of a good standard the chances of these structures being used are very remote. They are very likely to end up just as a hole in the earth or, at best, as storage sheds for wood or straw, just as government-funded toilets under the TSC have (see Photo 2.2). Providing low-cost toilets that are not used has no effect on faecal-oral disease and people's health; the economy will still suffer from the same number of man-days lost to sanitation-related disease. Gram Vikas believes that what is needed are cost-effective, not low-cost, solutions; low cost is an added advantage but should not be a precondition. Gram Vikas makes available to the poor toilets that are fit to be used. The logic is simple: 'We only build toilets that we ourselves would use.' (Gram Vikas, 2006a)

To avoid reinforcing long-held beliefs that the marginalized are not as important as others, Gram Vikas insists that each household is offered identical, good-quality facilities and so it promotes twin-pit pour-flush toilets to all households (see Appendix 3 for a description of this type of sanitary hardware). This is another step in raising the self-esteem of the poorer sectors, challenges any belief that they are undeserving, and helps to start breaking down social barriers. Providing a piped water supply to toilets is also seen as critical by Gram Vikas, since the burden of fetching water rests almost solely on the women, and in order to cover toilet usage women would need to fetch even more water than was needed before if water was not piped to toilets.

It is unusual for a water and sanitation programme to include bathing rooms; however, a bathing room ensures that people can bathe properly in privacy, which is particularly important for women. It was found that a number of skin diseases, such as scabies, spread rampantly during the summer months when the water level in ponds went down and people had to bathe in turbid water. The bathing room with a piped water supply dramatically reduces the incidence of such skin diseases, and is an integral part of the RHEP's design.

Photo 3.2 shows a typical layout of RHEP infrastructure in a village, in this case Samiapalli, with a toilet and bathing room block and kitchen garden behind each house. The water tank is located somewhere close to the village and supplied, commonly, from a protected open well. Samiapalli also uses a tube well for water supply.

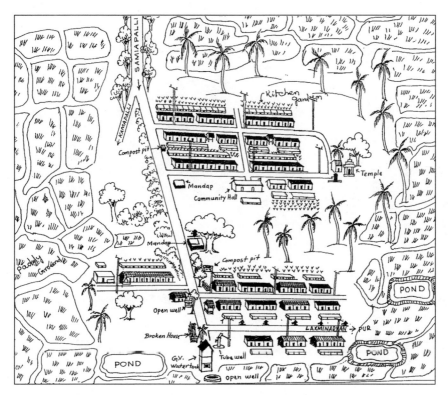

Photo 3.2 Map of Samiapalli, showing typical layout of RHEP infrastructure
Source: Gram Vikas.

CHAPTER 4
Initiating the RHEP

This chapter outlines the project cycle and Gram Vikas's structure for managing the programme. It looks at how new habitations for the intervention are identified, and details how Gram Vikas motivates villagers to implement the programme.

Project management structure and project cycle

Gram Vikas is represented in the RHEP villages by village volunteers and project supervisors. A village volunteer works only in one village and the supervisor facilitates the implementation in several villages at one time. The projects and supervisors of a region are in turn supervised by a project coordinator and his staff in the regional project office, which consists of an accountant and an assistant for planning, monitoring, evaluation and documentation (PMED). The RHEP manager and his assistant in the head office coordinate the efforts of the different RHEP project offices. Most staff at the head office also support the RHEP and ITDP through accounts, PMED, training, electronic data processing and purchasing departments.

Table 4.1 illustrates a typical plan for an RHEP project.

Identifying new project areas

The RHEP typically spreads through a demonstration effect. Leaders from villages which Gram Vikas supports become ambassadors, influencing neighbouring villages and nearby areas where they have relations or are hoping to build relations through marriage.

Gram Vikas also spread their work to new areas, especially to the underdeveloped and tribal areas, when it feels that there is a cooperative leadership and that people would possibly be willing to support the programme. It already has a good idea of the type of leadership and the attitudes of people in different villages from its work in the 1980s promoting biogas all over Orissa. Government officials (civil servants) and people's elected representatives also help Gram Vikas to identify new villages, and the leaders of those villages, in their respective areas. To date most of Gram Vikas's development has been in marginalized areas, that is, the south, south west and northernmost areas where there is a predominance of an *adivasi* population.

Table 4.1 Project plan for Gram Vikas's water and sanitation programme

---

Preparatory phase

Identify habitation and/or leaders

Make initial contact with leaders/elders

Meet with interested groups/leaders/elders

Meet more families (in the home); ongoing motivation; form SHGs

Meet all male and female heads of households (village general body); get 100% agreement to implement the programme

---

Implementation phase

Form the VEC from the village general body; sign MOU/Agreement between Gram Vikas and VEC

Form system management structures (committees for sanitation, water, health and education)

Ongoing training of all committee members in roles/responsibilities and relevant management skills

Ongoing motivation of inhabitants; regular meetings of village general body, VEC and sub-committees with support from Gram Vikas

Register the VEC and apply for *Swajaldhara* funds

Start collecting the corpus fund (possibly paid by instalments)

Conduct a baseline survey

Collect stones, sand, aggregates for foundations and soakpits of toilets/bathing rooms

Make bricks for construction

Masonry training

Construct foundations and soakpits of toilets/bathing rooms

Open a bank account and deposit the corpus fund

Buy/collect materials for superstructure of toilet/bathing rooms; finish construction

Conduct a hydrogeological survey

Identify land for the water tank; register the sites of the water tank and water source in the VEC's name

Dig open well(s) and/or drill tube well(s)

Collect materials for construction of the water tank

Construct the water tank

Lay the pipelines; on-the-job training of village youth in plumbing and electricity

Connect the electricity and establish running water to individual households

---

Evaluation

Ongoing monthly monitoring; additional training if necessary

Official withdrawal of Gram Vikas from management structures one year after commissioning of water supply; ongoing support available

---

Source: Gram Vikas.

There are three coastal districts in which Gram Vikas has done little or no work in connection with the RHEP: the erstwhile undivided Cuttack, Puri and Balasore districts, where by Orissan standards the people have a high level of education. The state leaders and administrators are mostly from those districts, and most of the Orissa development funds are routed there and because these districts already get most of the privileges Gram Vikas has tended not to work there. However, its view on this is changing and now it believes it is important to have at least some demonstration villages in those coastal areas within 30–40 km of the main city and airport at Bhubaneshwar, so that it will be easy for government leaders to make quick visits, since neither central nor state government officials want to travel far on poor roads. Once convinced of the effectiveness of the programme, Gram Vikas can get these leaders to use their influence and make policy changes.

Motivating villagers to join the RHEP

The preparatory phase begins with a series of meetings with the community leaders (always men). During these opening meetings Gram Vikas talks about health issues, women, their income, the environment and the RHEP and how it can help them generate more income. As soon as Gram Vikas feels that the programme is likely to be adopted by the village, its staff start to work intensively with the people to ensure they are fully motivated and reach a consensus. (For details on the actual methods used to motivate people to join the RHEP see pp. 46–9.) A village general body of the headmen and headwomen of each household is formed. Gram Vikas holds meetings with this body to speak about the issues mentioned above, what the RHEP can do for them, the terms and conditions (norms) of the RHEP, and what a formal Agreement between Gram Vikas and the community involves. Within the broad framework of the RHEP rules, the norms are negotiated with the village general body and adjusted to suit the village's circumstances, for instance, how the corpus fund will be raised, how the landless will get space for a toilet/bathing room, how the village will fund O&M costs, what type of water source will be used (spring or ground water). During these negotiations conflicts are resolved and the fact that the majority of Gram Vikas's project office staff are drawn from the local area helps smooth negotiations. When the village general body has finally reached a consensus and agree to implement the RHEP, a written Agreement detailing what Gram Vikas will do and what villagers will have to do is legally drawn up and paid for by the villagers. Every family signs this formal Agreement.

This preparatory phase took between two and three years in many of the early villages (sometimes longer), but generally takes between three and six months nowadays. Sometimes the negotiations are delayed because of Gram Vikas's insistence on women's participation in decision-making.[11] Participation by all headmen and headwomen of households is considered critical to the RHEP's aim of bringing people together and cutting through barriers of gender, caste, politics and economic differences. Box 4.1 describes how consensus was finally reached in one village.

Setting up the village general body

'When we are doing the intervention the women are shy – they are forced to be shy by their men' (Gram Vikas, 2006a). Because rural communities in Orissa are dominated by patriarchal attitudes, separate men's and women's general bodies are formed first, to allow the women to gain experience of speaking in front of large groups (this process is described below). Separate meetings go on for between about four and six months usually, until women feel confident enough to come to a joint meeting and voice their concerns in front of the entire village, and men begin to show a greater acceptance of women's opinions. At that point the two bodies merge into one village general body (see Photo 4.1).

Box 4.1 Reaching consensus in Mohakhand village – finally

Mohakhand village in Bargarh district has a population of 158 households, mostly engaged in agriculture and allied activities. The village had many problems such as scarcity of safe drinking water, a general lack of awareness regarding health and sanitation, and the common practice of defecation on the sides of the road and near water sources. The villagers invited Gram Vikas to discuss the possibility of implementing the RHEP as a way to eradicate these problems and improve their living conditions. Initially many people in the village were very interested, but there were a few families who were not ready to participate, so 100 per cent consensus could not be reached and the programme was not implemented. The interested villagers did not give up and some months later they again approached Gram Vikas, but a consensus could still not be reached.

In the meantime the RHEP was successfully implemented in the nearby village of Karnapalli, which originally had all the same problems as Mohakhand. After witnessing the dramatic improvements at Karnapalli, the villagers of Mohakhand, especially women, were inspired once more to urge for the implementation of the RHEP in their village. A delegation of spirited and energetic women from Mohakhand went to meet the RHEP programme manager, who was visiting Karnapalli, and expressed their desire. The programme manager was reluctant at first, as twice before the villagers had requested the implementation of the programme but could not come to a consensus. However, the women were insistent and said that if the men did not cooperate they would go for an indefinite kitchen strike to ensure their cooperation, and they would employ outside labour for the construction of the RHEP infrastructure. The women's commitment was overwhelming and made the programme manager feel confident that the village was at last ready to undertake the RHEP.

Photo 4.1 Meeting of a village general body
Source: Gram Vikas.

It is this village general body which decides whether the village will take part in the RHEP or not. If even one family says no, Gram Vikas will not implement the programme. Gram Vikas says: 'The advantage is that if you persuade the majority of the village they will put pressure on the others: those that do not see the light will not be allowed to draw water from this well; if their daughter gets married the others will not go to their house to celebrate the wedding.' (Gram Vikas, 2006a)

Once the Agreement has been signed and the RHEP is being implemented the general body will continue to meet every month to examine accounts, discuss progress and any issues arising.

Involving women: setting up SHGs and the women's general body

Sometime around the fifth meeting between Gram Vikas and the village (village leaders and their supporters mainly at this early stage), Gram Vikas tells the men that the women must also be involved. The women bear most of the health responsibilities: they are the ones who care for the sick, they prepare the food, they mind the small children, so they have to understand the implications of open defecation and poor hygiene, otherwise they will allow the children to defecate wherever they please and faecal-oral disease will remain prevalent.

Orissa is a very conservative state and women do not normally leave the house other than for chores. Gram Vikas put a lot of effort into getting the women to venture out of the house, and also into giving them the confidence to speak out (see Box 4.2). On the men's agreement, Gram Vikas' female extension workers start contacting the women on a house-to-house basis, and they sit together and talk.[12] From there the extension worker sets up small SHGs and educates the women about savings and credit and sensitive issues relating to health (including gynaecological health), sanitation, hygiene, family planning, looking after children and immunizations.[13] The SHGs meet approximately once a month, giving women a reason to leave the house. In this non-threatening environment women make contact with each other and discuss their problems; they are free to voice their opinions and gradually they gain confidence in public speaking.

At the SHG meetings the women start saving and are also taught about managing money. The amount saved depends on the capacities of the people involved. In some groups each member saves only INR10 a month, some groups save INR30 a month each. The groups get schooling in reading and writing, and how to fill in bank forms, and their leadership skills are developed. Before the formation of SHGs most women had never gone to the bank unless accompanying their husbands; the idea of speaking directly to the bank manager is frightening. Through capacity-building, including financial training from local bank managers (coordinated by Gram Vikas), they gradually lose their fear and what was previously inconceivable becomes business as usual. Women are no longer dependent on the men to manage their

---

Box 4.2 Getting women to come out of the house

'In the past we knew nothing – no guts to speak out. Stepping out has given us a world of confidence. That's power!' [Woman speaking on the film *100%* (Gram Vikas, 2003a)] In Samiapalli (one of the five pilot villages) an older woman related how the project coordinator talked to each woman individually and explained to her what the benefits of the RHEP were: 'He created a picture that was quite tempting, something I'd never imagined.' He gave her some exercises in reading and writing every day. For almost a year he encouraged her 'just come to the door', 'come sit outside the house', 'why not come stand at the community meeting, you don't have to sit with the men you can sit on the other side; no need to make any decisions, just come and observe', and so on. So the project coordinator pushing them to take these little steps, and partly their own curiosity, finally got the women attending meetings.

Even though it took nearly a year for the women of Samiapalli to leave their houses and come and join the meetings, Gram Vikas said it was not going to take any steps with the RHEP until the women were fully involved. From the time that the women joined the general body it took two months to get all the men and women to agree to take up the RHEP in that village.

affairs; they are able to take care of all aspects of their group activities for themselves.

Whereas anybody can be a member of a SHG, the women's general body is made up of only the headwomen of every household. This group meets separately once per month for between four and six months, by which time the women feel confident enough to meet the men in the village general body. Initially women from different castes will sit on separate mats and there is not much interaction, but with encouragement from Gram Vikas's extension worker they come to understand that they must work together or else Gram Vikas will not implement the RHEP. Thus clean, running water is used as the key to the process of breaking down barriers. Once women learn how the RHEP can improve their lives, it is typically they who are active in getting the 100 per cent support needed for the RHEP to be initiated. (See Box 4.1 for the story of how the women of Mohakhand village agitated for the RHEP to be implemented.) Bit by bit they become readier to take part in discussions with men and make decisions. When the village has decided to implement the RHEP, women's SHGs often assume responsibility for development activities like monitoring village cleanliness, attendance at school and health (immunizations and growth rates). One woman explained that her SHG is 'a great way to catch up with news, and plan the next project ... and there's always much more to be done'.

Formulating a plan for funding operation and maintenance

Before the Agreement is signed each village has to find ways to sustainably cover the O&M costs (pump operator's wages, ongoing maintenance and the electricity bill for pumping) of their proposed water supply. The village covers these costs through a combination of using community funds and monthly contributions by individual households. The monthly contribution is for the electricity bill, since Gram Vikas believes that unless villagers feel the pinch in their pockets they will not associate excess water usage with expense, and will be wasteful. The monthly fee is fixed by the villagers themselves, with the poorer people paying less than the better-off; this is equitable because poorer households tend to use less water. The contribution is generally INR20–30 per household per month.

The community fund is used to pay the other expenses associated with the water supply (wages, spare parts, general maintenance costs). Gram Vikas helps villagers to identify potential sources of community income such as from social forestry, community horticulture on wastelands, fish farming in village ponds. Once an income source is identified the villagers must develop the asset and manage it efficiently. Gram Vikas advises on this, but it is the villagers' responsibility. In villages which have no community income-generating resources – for instance, if all land is under agriculture – people contribute a certain percentage of their gross product (harvest) to the community fund. This is considered by Gram Vikas to be fair since the landless will not be liable for this contribution.

Motivational methods used by Gram Vikas

Gram Vikas says that it is relatively easy to convince people of the advantages of having clean water at the turn of a tap, but it is still not easy to convince them of the need for sanitation. So it works on the principle of getting people to agree to join up for the clean running water and from the start tell them that they will get running water only on completion of sanitation. It is a bit of a strong-arm tactic but the truth of the matter is that if Gram Vikas did not insist on toilets before water it would take a very a long time to end the centuries-old practice of open defecation, and rampant disease would remain a feature of life. Kar (2003) reports that one village in Bangladesh used the same tactic of sanitation before water to ensure that everyone built a toilet.

Gram Vikas works at motivating villagers all the way through the project cycle. 'While we are implementing the programme we are saying "Why protect the water?", "Why build the toilets before the water?", "Why wash hands?". it takes a lot of repetition, and is an ongoing thing.' (Gram Vikas, 2006a)

Informal discussions

There is no formula for how Gram Vikas motivates people: each village and person have different problems. It has found that getting people in small groups and informal settings, like having a cup of chai at the tea stall, and then just informally dropping into conversation about health and sanitation works much better than formal meetings. They first approach the village leaders: 'Hello sir, come have some tea, sit down have a chat', and talk about health issues, asking questions like 'Last year how many of your people got diarrhoea? How many got jaundice?' This is followed up by explaining that open defecation leads to the spread of diseases such as cholera, diarrhoea, typhoid and jaundice, and appealing to people's sense of propriety by asking, 'Is it right that people in the 21st century live like this and dirty the place?'. They explain that having toilets would mean better health and that the women would not have to go out to defecate before everyone else woke up; that having running water would mean that the women would save a lot of time in fetching water from far away and they would be able to do other things with this time. It is hoped that these preliminary talks open the doors for further discussions with women in the houses. Without the man's agreement it is not possible to talk to the woman.

Once inside each house it is important to find a way of approaching the hygiene subject, and it is best if it is something that directly affects that household so that the discussion is about them. For instance, if there is a child that is sick talk about that illness. Gram Vikas has its own staff artists who create posters depicting relevant hygiene and social issues and the workers use these to help convey relevant messages.

This sort of motivation involves a lot of talking to individuals; by itself it does not make a serious impression, but it does break the ice.

Exposure visits

The most effective motivator is when people can visit a village that has already implemented the RHEP. They see this other village transformed into something completely different from their village.[14] Exposure visits happen at different times during the motivation, depending on who needs convincing at what point. In the early days it took a lot of time to build up the villagers' trust because they are afraid of corruption and they do not believe anybody; now it is easier to convince people because they can talk to other villagers and see how the RHEP works in practice. The first men approached by Gram Vikas are the village leaders, and it is hoped that when these leaders start trying to convince others their status will have a strong positive influence and other households will follow their lead. Once two or three households are convinced to join the RHEP they then help to persuade more villagers.

Film and video

Since 2003 Gram Vikas has also been showing the film *100%* (Gram Vikas, 2003a) to villagers early on in the intervention, and that has helped enormously in speeding up motivation.[15] Discussions held about the film help to clarify concerns and doubts that the community may have had about the RHEP or Gram Vikas. On one occasion the film was being shown in a particular village; a few people from another village happened to be there and saw the film and they were also motivated to join the RHEP. This is one of the ways in which the programme is now spreading.

In 2005 *100%* was shown on local TV, and the project coordinators from Ganjam and Mayurbhanj districts took part in radio programmes with regional All India Radio stations. Gram Vikas says that many people had already heard about the RHEP, but seeing and hearing about it in the media was like an endorsement – like it was now official. This media exposure has led villagers to approach Gram Vikas and ask to be part of the RHEP: Mayurbhanj district alone has a minimum of 10–15 villages approaching them every year.

Influential experts

Since 1998, Gram Vikas has been conducting health camps in locations where there are clusters of tribal villages, with presentations and posters about children's health and the link to water and sanitation. A doctor does stool tests to show the people all the parasitic worms that are inside them; the doctor also does stool tests on villagers who have implemented the RHEP and shows the difference between the two. The tribals have a blind belief in doctors, so this really impresses them. The doctor tells the people that the parasites are a result of poor hygiene, and that to avoid getting them people need to use a latrine and stop defecating in the open, and wash their hands with soap before touching food and after defecating.

Some religious leaders can also be a help in motivating people. Gram Vikas has found that Christian leaders will talk to people about diseases and hygiene issues, and ignite thoughts of development alongside promoting religious beliefs. Hindu leaders tend to be mainly interested in igniting people's faith.

Drama

In Ganjam district Gram Vikas uses drama to show the evil bugs that affect the body. During leadership training events for the villagers plays and skits on topics like 'What happens if you don't wash your hands with soap after you go to the toilet?' 'What is RHEP aiming to achieve?' are enacted, with villagers acting out a role-play. Any drama is linked to the message they are trying to get across at a particular time – be it health, women's empowerment, whatever. Social dramas are adjusted to the situation and depict all stakeholders involved, so that people can relate to the characters.

Other methods

Gram Vikas also uses some other approaches to help convince people of the need to change their practice of open defecation. These are as follows.

Take a glass of water, stir in some cow dung and ask the people to wash their hands in even a tiny bit of this water – this disgusts them. 'But this is what you're bathing in every day!' They realize that they are actually bathing in faeces; they are using this contaminated water when they pray to their gods; they wash their clothes in it and then go to the temple. This simple action makes them see what they are doing. Before this, despite what Gram Vikas said, they still thought that the excreta of the buffaloes did not really affect them.

Get the villagers to take the Gram Vikas worker on a walk through the village to see the defecation spots. This is a very shaming experience for the inhabitants; they do not want to linger near those parts. After they have walked fully through the village, get the participants to draw a map of the defecation sites. Then they come to realize just how filthy their village is. This method is similar to the 'walk of shame' used by the Village Education Resource Centre's (VERC) TSC in Bangladesh, as described by Kar (2003).

Talk to pupils in school and show them the films *100%* and *The Samantrapur Story* (Gram Vikas, 2003a). Children are open-minded and willing to try out new things, so when you show them something they want to copy it. They will bring the message home and tell their parents of the possibilities under the RHEP.

CHAPTER 5

Project implementation, monitoring and evaluation

This chapter describes the process of managing, constructing, monitoring and maintaining the infrastructure relating to the programme. This is followed by a look at the indicators used by Gram Vikas in monitoring and evaluating progress. The final section itemizes some changes that have been made to the implementation process through time, as a result of lessons learned.

Setting up the Village Executive Committee and sub-committees

The development of community-based management systems is vital to allow for the eventual withdrawal of Gram Vikas, and empowering communities to effectively plan, implement and monitor progress is a cornerstone of the RHEP. After the Agreement is signed, the men's and women's general bodies nominate and select four men and four women from among themselves to form a representative committee, the Village Executive Committee (VEC), which has final responsibility for implementing the programme. The VEC also has proportionate representation of all sections of the community (SC, ST, landless, small and marginal farmers, etc). The VEC stays in place for three years and then the people have the opportunity to re-elect the same people or elect different representatives.

One of the first acts of the VEC is to register itself under law as a village society. This enables the committee to become legally recognized and helps in dealing with outside agencies, especially government agencies. It is a necessary step to allow more effective leveraging of government funds (e.g. *Swajaldhara* funds); the legally recognized status enables the body to enter into agreements and undertake financial transactions.

Various sub-committees are elected to support the VEC and manage particular development activities, for instance committees for sanitation, water, health, education, and (if a pond or social forest is available) fish farming and forestry. These sub-committees meet once a week. While the water and sanitation infrastructure is being built the VEC meets at least once a week, in the presence of whichever sub-committee it wants to chivvy along or get updates from. Thereafter the VEC must meet at least once a month, but depending on the need it may meet more often.

A meeting of the village general body and the elected committees is held at least monthly (more likely to be fortnightly) to discuss progress, problems, future plans and accounts. Details of major activities, expenses and contributions by the people are put on public display in each village, thus sharing information and maintaining transparency.

Gram Vikas continually works on building the people's capacity, with training sessions, workshops and practical support. At the start of the intervention all committee members go through leadership-development programmes and are trained in record-keeping (accounts). Other capacity-building includes gender sensitization, health training and training in dealing with the PRI. In the beginning Gram Vikas gives a lot of assistance in running meetings and managing construction, until leaders' confidence is built up. Despite the initial difficulty in involving women, their raised confidence as a result of involvement in SHGs means that they play a key role in implementing and managing the various aspects of the RHEP. Over time the villagers gradually take on more responsibility; eventually the whole system becomes self-governing. A typical project lasts between three and five years, after which Gram Vikas withdraws and the community takes full responsibility for the management, operation and maintenance of all systems.

Collecting and banking the corpus fund

After the initial mobilization of the people, Gram Vikas looks for a firm commitment from people that they are going to put efforts into making the RHEP work. The monetary commitment of INR1,000 on average from each family to a community corpus fund is the acid test. Gram Vikas will not start implementing the RHEP until the corpus fund is collected. Exactly how villagers come up with the corpus fund money is described on pp. 98–100.

The fund is deposited in a fixed-deposit account, with the VEC president and secretary as signatories, together with the executive director of Gram Vikas. Partial control by Gram Vikas is only for the first five to seven years to ensure that the fund is not embezzled or misappropriated in some way. In some villages collection of instalments to the corpus fund may start even before the Agreement is signed, if the villagers trust their leader with the money.

Conducting a baseline survey

Soon after the Agreement is signed a once-off baseline survey of the village is conducted by Gram Vikas's RHEP field supervisors, who are trained in interviewing, observing and recording techniques. Each head of household, male or female, in a village is interviewed (subject to their consent) in a language that they understand, and a structured questionnaire relating to the household is completed by the interviewer. Interviews are held at the respondent's house at a time that suits the householder, usually either the morning or evening. Each interview lasts approximately one hour, but it can be staggered over more than one sitting if necessary. Most of the data collected relate to factual household characteristics, and data collection is mostly via close-ended questions, noting down figures, ticking options; but some opinions are also sought, and interviewers are asked specially to note down any culture-specific or unusual phrases used by respondents. All data collected are held strictly confidential. Questionnaires are edited by the interviewer as soon as possible after the interview, to ensure completeness and uniformity; if necessary the interviewer returns to the household to clarify any gaps in understanding; the interviewer also notes his/her personal observations in a field notebook at this time. Data are analysed later on in head office using both quantitative and qualitative approaches.

Household data are collected on topics such as demography; caste; occupation; land-holding; finances (income, expenditure, savings, loan/ credit status); access to electricity, biogas energy, government food rations; housing (including sanitation and water supply used); food sufficiency and nutrition; health (diseases suffered, births, deaths, immunizations); education and children's school attendance.

The aim of this baseline is to provide a benchmark against which an objective assessment of the outcomes and impacts of the RHEP can be made, particularly in the areas of health, financial stability and education. It is important to gain the trust of respondents, and doubly so if honest answers regarding finances are to be obtained. The rural poor of Orissa have a long history of exploitation at the hands of moneylenders and are wary where finances are concerned.

Constructing toilets, bathing rooms and the water supply

Once the corpus fund has been collected and all the committees are set up, people can start the foundations and brickwork for the toilets and bathing rooms (water-related construction only starts when sanitation work is finished). Gram Vikas's experts will already have provided an infrastructure layout (with the assistance of the community) as soon as it looked fairly certain that the village will implement the RHEP and before the Agreement is signed.

Gram Vikas provides master masons for training local youth as masons (mason training is described on pp. 79–81) and for supervising construction work. Because Gram Vikas was finding it difficult to motivate and retain qualified engineers to live and work in remote rural areas, it also started a barefoot-engineers training programme in 2002. The aim of this programme is to develop a body of trained people to carry out basic engineering tasks at the village level, living in the villages and supporting the construction work. The barefoot-engineering programme is integrated with mason training.

Sanitation technology

As explained on p. 36, Gram Vikas promote only good-quality sanitation; all villagers build pour-flush twin pit latrines.[16,17]

Everything is ready for a quick start with the building, since the villagers will have been gathering stones, sand and other local materials in preparation before the Agreement was signed. People make the bricks, or buy them if suitable material is not available locally. Toilets and bathing rooms are constructed at least 3 m away from the house if possible to avoid issues with lack of cleanliness, because of an initial inhibition about having toilets near the house. This distance also allows for the future extension of the house if required. In some areas of the state the houses are railway-carriage (terrace) style, and having 3 m between the back windows and the toilet building allows light into the house. To avoid the flooding of latrine pits during the rainy season (due to surface-water influx), the tops of the platform and the pits must be 0.45–0.6 m above ground level (see Photo 5.1).

Photo 5.1 Side-view of toilet building showing raised plinth and pits
Source: Gram Vikas.

When the walls are complete up to roof level Gram Vikas provides the INR3,000 social-cost subsidy (explained on pp. 33–4), and BPL families get their TSC subsidy. Villagers can use the subsidy money to buy the components required to complete the construction (pan, door, cement and steel for the roof). Gram Vikas buys these materials in bulk and passes the dealer's price on to villagers, thus getting them at a better price than they could get on the open market. The costs associated with sanitation are described on p. 97.

Identifying a suitable water source

A suitable water source needs to be identified and the most appropriate source will depend on local conditions. For all water supplies issues of ownership of the source and the land on which the source is sited and through which the pipeline must pass need to be investigated and ironed out.

In the plains areas Gram Vikas generally tries to use protected dug wells rather than drill deep tube wells: to ensure sustainability of the source it is necessary to recharge the aquifer with at least as much water as is taken out, and it is much easier to recharge shallow unconfined aquifers. (Aquifer recharge is discussed further on p. 59.) However, in some areas dug wells are just not possible and deep tube wells must be drilled, like in Bolangir where the water table is roughly 75 m below ground level.

In the more remote, and poorer, hilly areas, over 90 per cent of the tribal villages that Gram Vikas works with do not have access to electricity. This poses a dilemma as Gram Vikas aims to ensure that all villages have access to a protected and piped supply of water. (Piped water is important because it has been found over time that toilets without a water supply, the kind usually built under government schemes, are ineffective and unused.) In a few villages, where feasible, the government is pursued to provide electricity. In other villages, especially in remote and inaccessible hilly areas, alternatives have to be found. The more conventional alternatives to pumping by mains electricity are diesel generator, or solar or diesel pump, all of which are currently more costly than mains electricity.[18] While they did consider these alternative means of generating power, Gram Vikas found that the optimal solution was gravity flow supply of water.

Water is channelled from a perennial spring, always using only a part of the spring's water flow. A spring box is built at the source and water is piped from there to a storage tank in the village, and then on to individual houses. The villagers take responsibility for maintaining the pipeline system. People contribute all unskilled labour, stone and sand, while Gram Vikas pays the cost of the pipeline, cement, masons, etc. Though the initial investment is high (depending on the length of the pipeline and the size of the storage tank), the recurring costs are negligible because gravity flow eliminates the need for a pump and its associated power and maintenance costs. During construction care has to be taken that: the pipes are well buried to prevent breakage; the area around the source is kept clean to prevent pollution of the water and ensure the pipes are not blocked by debris; the entire micro-watershed around the source of the spring is maintained under tree cover to slow down surface-water run-off, encourage groundwater recharge and prevent the spring from drying up.

Water tank and supply system

After the toilets and bathing rooms are completed it usually takes about three months to complete the water supply. Gram Vikas's aim is to have running water available at the turn of a tap. They design the water supply so that 35–40 litres per person are stored in a raised community water tank and water can be pumped to the tank twice daily, giving up to 70 litres per person per day. Water flows from the tank under gravity to the houses. Each house is provided with three taps: one each in the kitchen, toilet and bathing room. When the toilets and bathing rooms are being built drainage systems are incorporated to ensure that wastewater does not accumulate.

All households contribute to the building of the water tank, in labour and in materials. The general body decides on the terms of contribution of free labour by all families. Villagers have to collect stone for the foundations and provide scaffolding for the construction work. The main pipeline is provided through government's *Swajaldhara* scheme funds, while the distribution pipes to individual houses are laid at the cost of the people. *Swajaldhara* funds around 70 per cent of the water supply costs.[19]

When built, the water tank is a distinctive landmark, painted a standard sandy-yellow with ochre/brown trim; it is instantly recognizable as a symbol of a village that is implementing Gram Vikas's RHEP and has running water and a toilet in every house. The water tower can simply be a tank on pillars, but Gram Vikas finds that a more popular design with villagers encloses the space below the tank, thus creating ground-floor and first-floor rooms with attached toilet and bathing facilities in the tower; water storage is at the top of the tower (see Photo 5.2). The two rooms are used as meeting places or as guest rooms. Having a guest room with its own private facilities means that government officials (civil servants) and elected representatives can visit and stay overnight, giving them time to interact with the villagers.

Photo 5.2 Water tower built under Gram Vikas's RHEP
Source: Gram Vikas

Water treatment

Gram Vikas tests the physical and chemical quality of the source water before the supply is connected: levels of arsenic, chloride, fluoride, hydrogen sulphide, iron, nitrates, sulphate, as well as the concentration of e-coli, are checked. To date, water from tube wells has not needed treatment. In a few areas the water is a little hard, but it is acceptable to the villagers. Water is treated before use by adding bleaching powder to the village storage tank (in the case of dug wells the bleaching powder is added to the well). The inside of the water tank is cleaned regularly by the villagers. Dug wells are covered to prevent contamination of the source. Spring water that is collected via a spring box may simply need passing through a silt trap before piping to the water tank.

Once the supply is connected the source water is sampled and tested approximately every three months during the dry season. (When open defecation in the surrounding area has stopped and people are aware of hygiene issues there is little risk of faecal contamination.) The water sample is collected from the source by the villagers and immediately sent to head office for an assessment of chloride, fluoride, hydrogen sulphide, iron and nitrates content. During the rainy season, the period when the source is most vulnerable to the infiltration of contaminants through flood water, the water is tested at least once per month.

Ensuring the sustainability of the water supply

An important aspect of the RHEP is that, having contributed around 30 per cent of the hardware cost of their water supply (see p. 97 for a breakdown of project costs), villagers have a strong sense of ownership of the system. This means they will look after their assets and will maintain them so that the system continues to work. This is borne out by the fact that all the systems, except a few, are still functioning well, even after 10 years in some instances. Potential methods of funding O&M are described on p. 45. See Box 5.1 for one villager's views on funding O&M.

When villagers first get continuous water supply there is commonly a lot of water wastage, for perhaps two or three months until people learn how to use taps correctly and make the association between wasted water and high electricity bills for pumping. The village water committee talks to households about conservation issues; if people use water for purposes other than for the household (e.g. for small-scale irrigation), they are liable to be fined because of the extra pumping cost unless a prior agreement has been made with the VEC regarding the amount of water they may use and the amount they must pay for pumping costs.

A pump operator is needed to keep the water system running smoothly and this person is paid a wage by the villagers from the O&M fund. In each village a few local youths (male and female) are trained as pump operators and learn how to repair most technical problems that are likely to arise. One person is selected by the villagers to look after maintenance and signs a contract to work for a certain number of years; at any time the villagers can terminate the contract if necessary and replace the pump operator. Generally speaking, married women are less likely to move away from their village than single men are, so training women as operators would seem like a better idea. Gram Vikas does train women but finds that during the summer months, when the electricity supply is commonly only available at night time, women do not like to be out attending to the pump, so male pump operators are also needed.

Box 5.1 Something always breaks...

When asked about funding O&M, the headman of Tamana village saw no point in speculating what he might do with the money if he didn't have to spend it on O&M. He said: 'O&M costs are a reality, we have to give the money – something always breaks. If we didn't have to give the money of course we'd use it for something else we need. We don't have luxuries, but we can send our kids to school – there's a school right here in the village. We don't have fancy food but we have enough. Medicine bills used to be very high, it is still there but it has come down – there is much saving on that. Before when people had any money they used to use it to drink, now they don't do that because they need to have this INR20 at the end of the month or else their water will be cut off.'

Of the 105 villages covered by the RHEP prior to 2003 all of the water supply systems are functional, with every household having piped water available round the clock to three taps. In one village the water supply is currently not operational due to the failure of a tube well and another well is being constructed in the village. There are also some villages where the electricity is very unreliable (they have a single-phase electricity connection), so water is not available 24 hours per day. The available options in these cases are: lobby government for a more reliable electricity service; buy a diesel generator or install a dug well with a diesel pump (capital outlay plus increased O&M costs); use a solar pump (high capital outlay); or revert to the old water sources (undesirable).

Gram Vikas does not assist in providing water for large-scale irrigation projects, but a few family groups have taken loans from the NGO in order to dig or drill a new well and set up irrigation systems for crop growing.

Aquifer recharge and watershed management

Up to 2003, tube wells were the preferred water source in RHEP projects as the government would only sanction tube wells as the source for water supply. However, Gram Vikas has found that chemical contaminants in the water have increased as a result of the practice of extracting fossil groundwater: arsenic, nitrates and fluoride are now found during sample analysis. Instances of tube well failure and concern for future sustainability have led Gram Vikas to increasingly use protected dug wells with appropriate aquifer recharge mechanisms, for example, building ponds and check dams to slow down water run-off and give it time to seep into the ground. Gram Vikas believes that we have the right to extract only as much water from the ground as can be replenished in the earth. In older villages that have tube wells, where the community can finance it, back-up sources are also being developed.

Table 5.1 highlights the change in preferred water source since 2003. Through their NGO networks, Gram Vikas are encouraging other NGOs to lobby government and engineering departments to refrain from using tube wells for water supply whenever an alternative is feasible.

Table 5.1 Water sources used in RHEP villages

	Total water supplies built	Water source			Dug well or spring as % of total
		Tube well	Dug well	Spring	
Pre-2003	105	95	5	5	9.5
Post-2003	260	156	39	65	40

Source: Gram Vikas.

Watershed management activities (including aquifer recharge) are being implemented in a few drought-prone areas where specific government funding is available for that purpose. Gram Vikas is using these government-sponsored projects as a learning ground, and plans to put the learning to use especially in vulnerable drier areas to ensure the sustainability of water sources. Bolangir district, in western Orissa, is one such dry area: although the area gets good rainfall during the monsoon the water is allowed to run off, leaving a very low water table. Gram Vikas feels that the solution for villages in this district would be to actively encourage aquifer recharge and raise the water table, use a dug well for water supply for as much of the year as possible, and when the well dries up resort to a tube well for the necessary two or three months. The problem with this solution is finding the financing for two different water sources.

Sanitation monitoring and penalties imposed by the community

'He who is not used to a toilet will need encouragement to make sure he uses it – this stage can take an awful amount of time, maybe a year' (Gram Vikas, 2006a). Gram Vikas does not insist on people using the toilets before the water supply is connected up: if there is a water source close by people may choose to fetch water to clean the toilets during this period, but generally speaking people will still practise open defecation. Once the water supply system is connected, the VEC together with the village general body lays down rules to ensure that people use the toilets; SHGs and schoolchildren inspect toilets and report any problems to the committee. The SDC reported in its assessment of the RHEP (2000) that there was no doubt that women played an important role in the successful acceptance of toilets. Many VECs, for example those of Tamana and Samiapalli, put in place a system of fines for unclean toilets and open defecation within 1 km of the village environs. This is done on the villagers' own initiative, not at Gram Vikas's insistence, and is an indication of villagers being ready to take control.

Through the sanitation committee villagers impose a fine for open defecation ranging from INR50 to INR500 and INR10–25 for a dirty toilet, depending on the village. That fine goes to the water supply O&M fund. Any person who reports to the sanitation committee that so-and-so defecated in the open on such a date also receives INR10 or INR20. Because of these social pressure tactics, people use the toilets and the village becomes free from open defecation. It can take a while to achieve 100 per cent sanitation. In Tamana people had to do a lot of pressurizing for a year on those who persisted with open defecation: 'It is not just about you, it is about our children's health'. In Samiapalli it took three or four months; in Neeladripur the men said they 'had no

Photo 5.3 Toilet and bathing room built under Gram Vikas's RHEP
Source: Gram Vikas.

choice' but to use the toilets from the beginning, since their women
folk pressurized them so much.

Environmental sanitation

Throughout the implementation process Gram Vikas educates people
young and old about environmental sanitation and hygienic behaviour,
encouraging them to adapt their ways and keep their village clean. The
sanitation committee monitors the general cleanliness of the village.
Regular cleanliness drives are carried out, with help from women's groups
and schoolchildren, to motivate villagers to ensure that the surroundings
are sanitary.

Occasionally villages have a problem with the drainage of excess
water, most commonly during the rainy season (usually between July
and September), and waterlogging occurs. Gram Vikas assists the VECs
of these villages to get government funding for the construction of
additional drainage channels so that stagnant water is not lying on
the ground.

Two villages in Bolangir have been awarded the *Nirmal Gram Puraskar*
(Clean Village Award) by the Government of Orissa. Nandiaguda GP, in
Ganjam district, was declared as *Nirmal Gram Panchayat* and received a
INR400,000 award from the president of India.

Ensuring the sustainability of sanitation

Villagers are encouraged to grow banana, papaya and coconut trees around toilet soak pits to leach excess water and keep the pits dry, so a pit can be used for at least five years before it becomes full and waste must be diverted to the other pit. By the time the second pit is full the contents of the first have been composting for a minimum of five years and are well rotted; even the most persistent excreta-related pathogens (*Ascaris* eggs, roundworms, and enteroviruses like hepatitis A and poliomyelitis) will have been killed. Thus far, villagers have had no qualms about handling this compost which does not smell; it can be used on the kitchen garden, thus recycling nutrients through the food chain. Gram Vikas says that in practice even after five years there is often very little matter in the soak pit, so to date very few pits have had to be emptied.

As explained previously, the interest on the corpus fund is intended to provide the social-cost subsidy to help new families in RHEP villages meet the costs of construction of toilets and bathing rooms. Up to mid-2006 123 toilets and bathing rooms had been constructed by new households in existing RHEP villages, with 10 more under construction. Some villages have left the corpus fund intact and instead have taken money from other community funds to subsidize toilets for new families: 'seeing the money grow, the village committee has decided to meet the cost of new toilets from a separate community fund and not touch the interest from the corpus. The corpus money gives the villagers an additional sense of security.' (SDC, 2000)

Monitoring and evaluation by Gram Vikas

After the connection of the water supply Gram Vikas remains with the people for a period of between six and eight months, reinforcing gender and social equity, and helping with capacity-building and livelihood generation. During this period the Gram Vikas worker will spend around 60 per cent of his/her time with the villagers, and the remaining time is spent in promoting the RHEP in surrounding villages with a view to implementing new RHEP projects.

Gram Vikas's PMED team is responsible for monitoring and evaluating the overall programme. Different levels of indicators are used for evaluation purposes; some of the key indicators are itemized in Table 5.2. Data for the indicators are sourced from monthly reviews, monthly and half-yearly progress reports, field observations, health and school records, qualitative interviews, records of SHGs, project beneficiary organizations (PBOs), and PRIs, and election results.

Regular monitoring is conducted through a monthly progress report (MPR) submitted by each of the projects to head office. The MPRs are very extensive and detailed; records are kept of attendance at village meetings, construction progress, O&M costs met, capacity-building (training) activities, community income-generating activities, SHG and community savings and links to external bodies and schemes, health (disease incidences, causes of death, immunization, growth monitoring) and education (enrolment and attendance at school, adult literacy). The RHEP manager and other head-office staff also visit projects regularly and during these visits they observe whether facilities are being used and maintained, and whether people keep themselves, their clothes and their surroundings clean. The MPRs are analysed and collated by the PMED team for internal evaluation of the RHEP. The accounts and finance sections of Gram Vikas's head office independently monitor each project's use of financial resources. The RHEP manager and the project coordinators use these data to assess how things are going, and take action if necessary.

Lessons learned by Gram Vikas and how the approach has evolved

The first major lesson learned by Gram Vikas was that the aims of the programme could actually be achieved. When Gram Vikas first proposed the idea to their donors and government officials none of them believed that a small NGO in Orissa would be able to do what the government had not been able to do. Nor did the villagers believe that it could be done. Gram Vikas believes that the approach works because a sense of ownership is created among the people. The collective efforts of the people, in making sure that the work in all households proceeds more or less at the same rate, succeed in mobilizing a community like nothing else has ever done, they say. They conclude that this is the only way of designing a programme that has many spin-offs far beyond merely providing toilets and water.

General lessons that Gram Vikas have learned through their years of experience include the following points.

- Clean drinking water is something that all households are interested in, and provision of water can be used very successfully as a lever, or carrot, for community action and full participation.
- By insisting that toilets are built before the water system is started a whole village can become sanitized at an early stage in the intervention, and health is rapidly improved. The necessity for water treatment is also reduced. Toilets before water is a very strong motivational tool for sanitation and it has implications for increasing rural sanitation coverage at least in India. Other effective motivational methods for sanitation include social marketing on the grounds of preserving women's dignity (not exposing themselves to others while answering the call of nature) and improved marriage prospects. Hygiene promotion is still needed to break

Table 5.2 Key indicators monitored and evaluated by Gram Vikas

Specific objective and effect indicators	Examples of output indicators
Strengthened management capacity of project beneficiary organizations (PBOs)	
Number of members	Number and type of PBOs formed and registered
Quality of people's (members') participation in planning and management	Number of leaders and office bearers trained
Volume of collective village funds	Amount and type of collective assets transferred
Quality of management of common resources	Number of annual/periodic elections (which institutions) hel
Quality of distribution of benefits between people	
Quantity and type of external resources accessed by PBOs	
Cases of joint action against upper caste/ class atrocities	
Improved position of women	
Percentage of women in PBOs	Number and type of women's groups formed, number of members
Proportion of women PRI candidates elected on own merit to different posts	Number of women trained for which kind of position in PBOs and PRIs
Volume of women's funds and quality of spending by women	Number of women and type of women's groups linked with (type of) institution
Amount of external funds accessed by SHGs	Number of women trained for income generation
Number and quality of initiatives taken by women to solve common village issues	Number of women/men reached during gender sensitization sessions
Quality of work division between women and men	
Wage levels for women and men	
Percentage of family properties or assets jointly registered	
Improved education and health situation	
Literacy levels among children and youth (15–30)	Number and gender of children enrolled in schools
Rate of girl child attendance in schools	Number and type of supplementary nutrition, medicines and play material at pre-school centres
Infant mortality rate, maternal mortality rate	Number of children immunized

Specific objective and effect indicators	Examples of output indicators
Number and extent of malnourishment among children	Number of children and mothers who received health check-ups per year; number of check-ups per child/mother
Rate of morbidity among children	Number of village health workers and traditional birth attendants trained
Rate of morbidity among adults	Number of toilets, bathrooms, water-supply systems constructed
Quality of maintenance and management of water supply systems	Number of water sanitation committees installed
Quality of maintenance and management of sanitation infrastructure	
Quality of maintenance and initiatives to improve existing houses	
Type and quantity of government resources accessed by people for basic services like housing, drinking water, education, health	

Improved non-farm income	
Income levels of participating members	Number of women exposed and trained on other income-generating activity
Number and type of sources of incomes for so many families	Number of people trained for work and wage equality
Number and amount of loans accessed by individuals and groups	
Number and type of profitable micro-enterprises	

Increased access to government policies, services and resources	
Number and type of NGO/PBO programmes supported by government and the funding amount for same	Number and type of linkages established
Level of participation of village communities in different tiers of *panchayat* like *ward sabha*, *gram sabha*, *palli sabha*	Number of PBO functionaries trained
Number, type and quality of development programmes undertaken by *panchayat*	
Number and kind of linkages between NGOs and PBOs and government institutions	
Type and quality of changes in government policies and guidelines at relevant levels	

Source: Gram Vikas.

the faecal and oral routes of disease transmission, but hygiene promotion by itself is not an effective motivational tool.

- Inclusion of all households, that is 'all or none', ensures 100 per cent sanitation from the outset.

- Inclusion of headwomen of all households (as well as headmen) in decision-making helps to empower them. Institutional mechanisms (the village general body, the VEC and sub-committees) help to ensure they are always included. Village women have shown themselves to be a very valuable resource in ensuring that the water and sanitation project is implemented and monitored effectively, and in the longer term this has empowered women to agitate strongly for further village development.

- Financial mechanisms must be put in place to ensure the sustainability of the service. It is important that people have a sense of ownership over it so that they will pay for its expansion and ongoing O&M costs. (The corpus fund ensures future expansion is affordable; providing materials and labour creates a strong sense of ownership; people contribute to an O&M fund.) Finances must be transparent so that trust is fostered; regular reporting to village institutions is needed.

- The poor only ever seem to be offered low-cost and low-quality solutions, apparently reinforcing their low self-esteem and widening the gap between the haves and have-nots. Building the same good-quality services for all irrespective of caste or wealth is a first step in raising the self-esteem of the marginalized, challenging their belief that they are less deserving and raising their sights and ambitions. Furthermore, low-cost solutions may not be the most cost-effective: unless toilets are fit to be used they will not be used, and disease will persist.

- The poor can and will pay for good-quality services, once they are shown ways of financing it. However, society at large has a social duty to meet at least some of the cost of providing the rural poor with basic services.

- Incorporating livelihoods training (fish farming, social forestry, masonry, plumbing, etc) as an integral part of the programme helps communities to meet project costs (construction, O&M costs) and to raise funds for ongoing development of the village; it also provides individuals with an extra source of income.

- Time spent in consensus-building and dealing with divisions in society pays dividends later when the community is united, empowered and works together on its own initiative for their own development.

Insistence on 100 per cent consensus requires a lot of time upfront in mobilizing different strands of society: getting women and lower castes to participate, and getting people to overcome their differences and agree to join the programme. Because people have to unite, they learn to work through their differences, leading to a more harmonious society; having united, people realize their strength as a unit and are empowered to go further. The marginalized sections, which were until now excluded from all spheres of society, find themselves becoming part of a collective effort by the whole community. Realizing that they can work together (for in most villages there is a conviction that they could never all agree on something) gives everyone a sense of achievement. Now tribal people (who are considered to be the most marginalized in the society), as well as others, are taking the initiative in tackling their village problems. Now men are starting to give importance to women.

Gram Vikas's intensive mobilizing approach pays off at the other end: 'all or none' and 'toilets before water' mean that the village becomes free of open defecation soon after the facilities are built, and health benefits are experienced at an early stage. Compare this with the VERC's TSC in Bangladesh (a sanitation project which is promoted as a successful model) in which the adoption of sanitation depends on people's sense of shame being triggered, or others pressurizing them into building a toilet; under that TSC it may take a long time before some households build a toilet, so health benefits will not be anything close to immediate, and may never be completely enjoyed.

Compared with the VERC's TSC, Gram Vikas's RHEP is expensive in time and money, but the villagers get much more than just water and toilets. Management by the community has definite spin-offs in strengthened leadership skills, transparency in transactions, improved social harmony through conflict management, the raised confidence of lower castes and women, and improved access to government development resources. The programme may not be low-cost, but it would seem that the costs are outweighed by the benefits: a few simple interventions go a long way in giving these people some self-respect. For the first time the poorest woman in the village feels that she has equal importance to the wealthiest person, her voice is heard and she can influence decisions.

After the evaluation of RHEP projects the following specific changes have been made in the programme approach.

During the pilot phase (1992–5) the RHEP did not include water piped to the toilet and house (there were no bathing rooms either); instead standpipes were provided for every five families. However Gram Vikas found that in some places women were deliberately blocking the toilets with stones. They were fed up with having to collect water from the standpipes to clean the toilets, so they sabotaged them so that they could not be used. Around the same time Gram Vikas was becoming wary that people would not be willing to pay regular contributions to O&M for this low-level water service (standpipes). On searching for alternative means of funding O&M, Gram Vikas realized that most villages have ponds which could be used for fish farming. Income from fish farming could help to pay for O&M costs, an improved service (water to the toilet) could be provided and the women would no longer have cause to block the toilets.

Once water was being piped to the toilets, bathing rooms were added to the programme. At first the bathing rooms were not roofed, but it was quickly realized that women still had to bathe in their full clothing because people on a higher elevation (or in trees) could see into the bathing room. All bathing rooms are now totally private.

When Gram Vikas first started implementing the RHEP, it tried to get the women to participate in the village general body and VEC right away; but this did not improve women's confidence and they did not really participate. After some time a separate general body, exclusively of women, was tried. They found that here the women opened up and began to participate and make decisions, so this idea is now incorporated and is the prime way of building women's capacities.

Initially, once around 60 per cent of the households had constructed the toilet walls up to the roof level, Gram Vikas started releasing the social-cost subsidy to those who were ready. They found that once some subsidy had been released people who were not that interested in toilets stopped building. To ensure that everyone completed building, Gram Vikas changed its policy and now no subsidy is released until all toilet walls are up to roof level and the two soak pits are complete and covered.

Through the implementation work in villages, Gram Vikas learned the best ways to handle uncooperative people. It was found that the work gets done much faster if people work in groups under supervision rather than each one working alone on his own toilet or bathing room. Looking at these groups, it was found that if some people were not supporting the group fully they were likely to be trouble-makers later on also. So it is important to keep everybody, but especially these people, motivated and to instil a spirit of cooperation. All of the activities, including women's empowerment and SHG development, require a lot of effort in motivation and team-building throughout the process. Neglect of one aspect will mean trouble later, so monitoring all angles of the programme is important.

Initially Gram Vikas's masons did all the building work because there were no masons available in the villages. Gram Vikas quickly saw that in some of the villages there was no work available and youths were idle much of the time, so they started training local youths in masonry. This created long-term livelihood opportunities for youths and also helped create a stronger sense of ownership of the facilities. Now wherever Gram Vikas goes for the RHEP it will train interested unemployed, or seasonally unemployed, youths.

Gram Vikas found that some villages are very poor in cash but they have plentiful materials available locally, and labour that they can provide to reduce the cost of construction. If the villagers agree, Gram

Vikas can put INR1,000 of the usual INR3,000 subsidy (per house) towards the corpus fund (providing ready cash where none is available), and later give a reduced subsidy of INR2,000 towards construction materials.

CHAPTER 6
Programme outcomes and impact

This chapter tries to assess the impact of the RHEP on the natural and human resources of communities, and whether or not the programme is a success. This assessment was made on the basis of field visits to specific villages, interactions with Gram Vikas's staff involved with the RHEP, and a review of Gram Vikas's data and documentation. Sectors looked at include: coverage under the RHEP; the extent to which people are empowered to further their own development, and to which social and gender barriers have been affected; livelihood activities being undertaken; changes in health indicators and the numbers of children going to school. Villagers' views on why they initially did not want to join the RHEP, why they did finally implement the programme and the benefits they have seen resulting from it are reported.

Sanitation coverage under Gram Vikas's programme

Map 6.1 shows the areas that have so far been covered by the RHEP. The RHEP was first implemented in 1992 through a pilot project with 337 families in five villages.[20] By 1995 the approach and processes had been firmed up and by the end of 1998 over 3,000 families (in over 40 villages in 11 districts) had been covered. Villages had varied socio-economic profiles; the common factor was that all were poor. As Table 6.1 shows, by 31 March 2007 almost 27,000 households in 362 villages were covered by the RHEP; in most villages covered more than 80 per cent of families are below the poverty line. All villages are still 100 per cent free of open defecation even after 10 years, and almost all water supplies are fully functional.

Table 6.1 Population covered by the RHEP as at 31 March 2007

Villages covered	No. of households				No. of people
	SC	ST	GC	Total	
362	3,234	7,876	15,830	26,940	147,368
	12%	29%	59%		

Source: Gram Vikas.

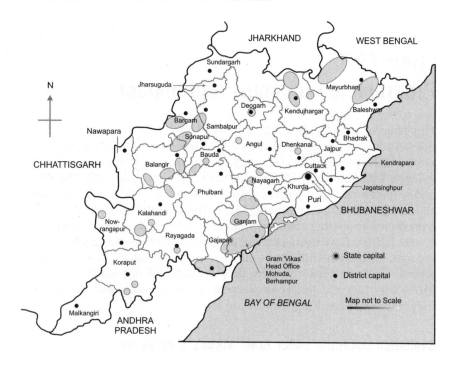

Map 6.1 Areas covered by the RHEP, as at December 2006
Source: Gram Vikas.

Capacity-building and community empowerment

When asked by the narrator of the film *The Samantrapur Story* (Gram Vikas, 2003a) what they thought the RHEP was about, villagers said: 'Awareness, savings, education for girls as well as boys, clean environment, income, childcare, economic growth, toilets and bathing rooms, political consciousness, self-reliance, women's rights, health, dignity, social growth, unity, water.' The RHEP is all about building progressive village communities. Sanitation infrastructure and a supply of piped drinking water all through the year to all houses is only the rallying element to bring people together, cutting through barriers of patriarchal systems, caste, politics and economic differences. Box 6.1 briefly describes life in Samiapalli before the RHEP was implemented, and after.

The big benefits of the RHEP approach are that villagers gain dignity and self-esteem, true leadership through their committee structures and a huge corpus fund which can be used as collateral against borrowing. The RHEP gives most villagers their first experience in managing their own village institution and financial resources, and helps build their abilities and confidence. Gram Vikas outlines clearly the villagers'

> **Box 6.1** Samiapalli: before and after the RHEP
>
> 'Samiapalli was one of the most divided villages we've ever come across – the people couldn't agree on anything, they had no community spirit. People had no jobs; they are all landless and of the lowest caste – the bottom rung on the ladder. They thought this was their lot in life and there was nothing they could do about it. Men were permanently drunk – drowning their sorrows in alcohol – and the women were getting beaten. Any little money that came in went on alcohol, so the village was in a pathetic state. [The villagers] never felt that they could pull something like [the RHEP] off together. And now they take their own steps, not with Gram Vikas pushing them. They've constructed a community hall and improved their roads, and they pay a tuition teacher to come and teach their children.' (Gram Vikas, 2006a)

responsibilities and rights; the initial period of hand-holding by Gram Vikas provides a safe environment in which communities can meet these responsibilities and experience democratic self-governance. The village general body meetings help to bring out the leadership, negotiation and organizational skills of people: villagers learn how to deal with conflicts and act as pressure groups against vested interests within their village and outside; they learn the ropes of organizing the village general body meetings and elections; they learn how to maintain public accounts and to question and hold accountable the VEC, which they elect. When people pay into the corpus fund and get (at least) monthly reports on accounts and spending, the accounts are posted up in the village for all to see and they realize that they can conduct business without corruption. This makes them more able to fight corruption in other aspects of their lives.

With the implementation of the RHEP there is a significant transformation in the living conditions of the villages; there is a real sense of a community investing in their own future. The surroundings are kept clean, village roads are levelled, water is not left to stagnate in cess pools. Villagers have self-monitoring mechanisms to ensure that toilets are kept clean. In time, when the people are comfortable with democratic self-governance and working together as a cohesive unit, they become confident and willing to tackle other development issues together. Several villages have gone on to build permanent houses after building permanent toilets and bathing rooms. After the villagers of Samiapalli had built their toilets and bathing rooms under the RHEP they saw that now their toilets were 'better than their houses', so people proceeded to relocate their village on land that it purchased through a bank loan, constructing *pucca* (permanent) houses. They also moved their toilets and bathing rooms brick by brick. When a massive cyclone struck Orissa in October 1999 the old village of Samiapalli was badly damaged, but the new houses were left intact. The SDC reports (2000) that the women find the *pucca* houses more convenient as they substantially reduce their maintenance workload.

The RHEP gives people a sound knowledge of accounting which helps them manage their village funds, and they also learn what good-quality work is. Previously if money came from local government for development work it would be given to contractors who did shoddy work and pocketed very large profits. After becoming united through the RHEP process villagers insist that they themselves carry out any development work. The work is organized by the village and they do good-quality work: some of their labour is paid, the rest of the contract money goes to the village fund. When a village is united and disciplined, projects are executed properly to a high standard. Government officials feel that this brings them credit, so they are happy to be associated with such projects.

Many villages have gone on to improve the management of other community services and resources, including the village school, health centre, common ponds and wastelands. Communities have accessed government funds to assist in building or improving roads, building schools and community halls, constructing ponds, etc. In an assessment of the RHEP conducted by the SDC (2000), it was found that Samantrapur village had started using the VEC to steer government programmes and that the village leader used the term 'development' with ease. Government funding to the tune of INR300,000 had been leveraged for the construction of the school building and the village road. This ability of the VEC to have an improved bargaining position to leverage finances from external agencies is, says SDC (2000), largely due to the RHEP. A 119 m² community hall had also just been completed in the village at a total cost of about INR280,000: around 45 per cent of the cost, or INR126,000, was raised by the villagers themselves (around INR38,000 in the form of labour and material, and INR88,000 from village funds).[21] The village committee had become a prime mover.

The SDC also reported (2000) that the young men of Karnapalli in Bolangir appeared to have obtained a strong sense of direction through the RHEP intervention. They aspired to make Karnapalli a self-sustaining place, thereby reducing the need to migrate for jobs. They also dreamed of 100 per cent literacy in the village, good roads, and houses with good lighting and ventilation. Their view was that there would be little need to migrate to towns and cities if their village itself were to have improved standards of living and an enhanced infrastructure.

Neeladripur villagers built a high school as soon as their water supply was completed, and everyone in the village pays towards the cost of the teachers. In the period 2005–6 over INR42m in government funding was sanctioned to 142 RHEP villages for non-water and sanitation work, over INR29m of which had been received.[22] This illustrates that villagers are able to successfully approach PRIs for funding. For the district administration Samiapalli is a model of rural development: the villagers say that the district collector (DC) pays a visit at least once a month.

Recently the DC sanctioned INR58,000 for the construction of a concrete road in the village; all proceeds from the contract will go to the village fund since the people are giving their labour free.

United villagers can see the strength of working as a group and this makes them more willing to approach PRIs to assert their rights to better service. To help villagers in their dealings with PRIs, Gram Vikas conducts awareness training and mock GP meetings. People gain a lot of confidence in dealing with the block development officer, collector and members of the legislative assembly (elected representatives). Gram Vikas encourages men and women who show leadership potential to participate in *panchayat* elections, because it sees that establishing links with the PRIs is an important step towards creating local government bodies that hear and respond to the people's needs. Most VECs have ward members or other *panchayat* representatives.

Gender and social equity

'It's unrealistic to think that improving access to safe water and sanitation can, by itself, eliminate poverty – a carefully planned and executed water and sanitation intervention can contribute to poverty alleviation only to the extent that it tackles associated dimensions of poverty, such as peoples' vulnerability, inequity and exclusion.' (Deverill et al., 2002)

Women are the obvious direct beneficiaries of the RHEP. Water piped to the house 24 hours per day spares them the drudgery of fetching and carrying water, and gives them more time to pursue productive activities like earning livelihoods and caring for children. Toilets provide privacy and convenience to women, sparing them the indignity of having to walk to potentially unsafe places in hours of darkness just to perform basic bodily functions. Bathing rooms eliminate the need to bathe (fully clothed and often in the presence of men) in contaminated ponds in which animals wallow. Yet even though the RHEP directly concerns them, because of age-old patriarchal customs women are at first reticent about taking part in community decisions regarding the RHEP – or anything else for that matter – until Gram Vikas assists them in coming out of the house (see Box 4.2). Under the RHEP women have an equal role in decision-making and system management: they begin to push for change. Women have taken over the responsibilities of maintenance and monitoring of water supply and toilets; they enforce the RHEP rules in the village and promote the RHEP beyond the village. They are also confident and firm in their interaction with officials, banks and other outsiders, and they are major players in resolving conflicts and organizing mass protests. In over 90 per cent of villages women's groups have taken initiatives to combat alcoholism, and during 2006 women organized anti-liquor rallies in several districts. International Women's Day is celebrated in all villages where Gram Vikas works.

Through involvement in planning, building and managing their water and sanitation systems, the marginalized sections of the community, who were until now excluded from all spheres of society, find themselves becoming part of a collective effort by the whole village. Irrespective of caste and wealth, all households have the same water supply system with three taps for each family (toilet, bathing room and kitchen) and the same-quality toilets and bathing rooms. This same-quality facility for all challenges the villagers' widely held belief that some are better than others; this is an important step in raising the self-esteem of the poor and lower castes. It takes a lot of time and energy to build the capacities of previously unrepresented, excluded sections of a village community. It also takes time for them to demand accountability from committee members, and for them to become dependable when in positions of responsibility. The SDC (2000) reported new patterns of leadership emerging in many villages in Ganjam, but that the rich and traditional leaders continue to influence decision-making. It is a slow process that can take between three and five years in order to get the people really taking on board the whole ethos of working together.[23] 'We must go slowly; otherwise we may feel we've achieved our goal, but we may not have the people fully with us, so it is not fully achieved.' (Gram Vikas, 2006a.)

Only eight of the villages that Gram Vikas worked with more than five years ago have run into gender equity problems. In those eight villages there is still 100 per cent sanitation, and new toilets and bathing rooms have been built for any new households setting up, but the men have said: 'Leave our women alone, you have done enough for them; if we need you again for anything we will call you.'

The fact that people are willing to treat each other as equals for the purposes of working on the RHEP, but not necessarily otherwise, is demonstrated on the film *100%*, in which a male villager says: 'The only time we involve women is for the RHEP work, and that's only because the rules say we must!'. And a young woman says: 'Gram Vikas may be here for four or five years, ask us to unite, but [caste] differences will remain,' Interestingly, this woman's husband did not think the caste barrier was as solid as it had been before the RHEP was implemented in their village. Perhaps men overcome the caste barrier more quickly than women? In Asuramunda village a higher-caste man said: 'We all had to sit together for meetings, and then as work came up we ended up doing it together. Now that's the way it is.' His SC co-worker agreed: 'No more caste bias ever since Gram Vikas came.'

While patriarchal attitudes that have remained unchallenged for centuries cannot be abolished in a few years, Gram Vikas claims that as a result of the RHEP there has been a loosening up of traditional roles and codes of conduct. This is probably true to a greater extent in the earlier villages, where the women have had time to work on the men and gain more freedom, and certainly in both Tamana and Samiapalli there are female *panchayat* members, which would have been unimaginable in those villages 10 years ago.

Livelihood creation

To be effective in reducing the vulnerability of rural communities, especially in times of disasters, it is vital that people have the capacity to take up livelihoods that provide sufficient income and allow at least a little to be saved on a regular basis. Gram Vikas promotes SHGs, skills-based training, fish farming, horticulture and small home industries based on forestry produce.

Tamana's headman is very proud that the village now has a grain bank and lends grain to the neighbouring Oriya village, where before they borrowed grain from that village at an interest rate of 50 per cent (if they borrowed 10 kg of grain they had to pay back 15 kg). This turning of the tables has greatly raised the self-esteem of these tribal people, since they would previously have been considered, and considered themselves to be, not as good as the Oriya villagers; but now they have a greater sense of worth. The headman says that because they have learned how to save money and put it to good use their children are now being educated, so they can get slightly better jobs than their parents, 'still not great but better'.

The GoI has designated approximately 200 districts nationwide as falling under the National Rural Employment Guarantee Act (NREGA); 12 districts in Orissa are designated. Under the scheme the GoI guarantees 100 days' employment to anyone in those districts who wants it; those who want employment get registered and are given a card which is checked off whenever they work. Workers are paid the minimum wage of the state in which they live, with equal pay for men and women for equal work. Local government officials run the scheme and the Act demands a separate village monitoring committee. However, it is open to corruption, as if people do not know their rights they may not get their full allowance. Gram Vikas informs people of their rights and, through their RHEP institutions, helps them to ensure the scheme works.

By 31 March 2007 a total of 362 villages were covered by the RHEP. The sum of their corpus funds totalled over INR33m. These funds are not allowed to be used as revolving funds, they must be allowed to gain interest and grow, but Gram Vikas envisages communities using the corpus fund as collateral for bank loans to start larger-scale businesses that will provide employment. Gram Vikas hopes that if this sort of larger enterprise starts up it would allow people to remain in the villages rather than having to migrate to cities for work. It is in fact hoping in the longer term to set in motion a process of reverse migration from cities to the villages. However, getting a larger business started up in rural villages will take some entrepreneurial skill and long-term mentoring by business experts, skills that Gram Vikas is not in a position to provide or fund at present.

Self-help groups

As explained on p. 43, Gram Vikas supports the formation and strengthening of SHGs, which are not just about savings and credit, but are also valuable forums for imparting information and increasing women's confidence. SHGs are not restricted to women, though the majority of the groups are women's groups. Groups typically consist of 10–15 members who agree to save a given amount each month. As the joint savings fund grows, members may borrow from it. Gram Vikas trains members in record-keeping and finances, and encourages members to undertake income-generating activities with loans from the fund. The SHGs grant loans at roughly 12 per cent interest, thus freeing people from having to take loans from unscrupulous moneylenders, who are known to charge a minimum of 36 per cent interest on the principal per month.[24]

As at March 2006, in eight of the districts covered by the RHEP (214 villages) there were 968 SHGs, with a total of nearly 12,000 members. On average 92 per cent of these members were female, with no male SHG members in some districts, but in Bolangir district 18 per cent of the members were male. These 968 SHGs had a combined value of INR18.6m.

Individual and collective income-generating activities that have been started with SHG funds include agriculture (dairying, fertilizer and pesticide selling), livestock rearing (poultry, goats, bullocks), fish farming, horticulture (mushroom, fruit and vegetable growing), forestry products (plate making and broom binding) and small shops (grocery, tailoring). See Box 6.2 and 6.4. The true indicator of the success of a savings-group is its ability to access external finances, and as each SHG gains ability and confidence it is linked to B-MASS (block-level Mahila Atma Sahayika Sangha: women's SHGs at block level), the government-sponsored SHG federation that facilitates loans through a government-established revolving fund. SHGs are also linked to local banks for external funds, which allows them to get into income-generating activities on a larger scale (Gram Vikas, 2006: 24).

Gram Vikas say that SHGs are 'fearless' as long as their Gram Vikas supervisor is there to support them, but in some groups suppressed internal conflicts rise again once their worker is no longer available. It may be that one person monopolizes the fund so that others cannot use it; or sometimes monitoring health and sanitation may not be as stringent as before. Gram Vikas says that it is important to ensure SHGs

---

Box 6.2 Rice and paddy business in Balimunduli, Mayurbhanj district

Balimunduli is a predominantly tribal village, and 41 of the 49 families are *adivasi*. Dependent on daily wage labour as farm workers, all families are BPL and often resort to borrowing money. Most of the men are alcoholics.

Gram Vikas started implementing the RHEP in the village in 1996. Seeing the success of women's savings groups started under the RHEP, 20 men in the village were encouraged to start a savings group of their own in 1999. Eleven of the men applied for a government scheme, Swarna Jayanti Gram Swarojgar Yojana (SGSY), to start a collective income-generation activity. The process involved a series of interactions with government officials and a bank; however, the bank officials were reluctant to lend money as the villagers had defaulted in the past. Gram Vikas stood as guarantor and the funds were released. The men were motivated to repay their dues to the bank and with the remaining amount they started business in sabai grass, rice and paddy. Though only 11 of the SHG members got the SGSY assistance, the fund was pooled among all 20 members and added to the savings of the entire group.

The 20 members collectively run the business activities, with a clear division of responsibilities. They keep separate records for stock, marketing and other group details. Profits are shared and provide additional income on top of the wages these men earn each day. The members who do not carry out their assigned responsibilities are fined INR20, which is deducted from their profit. They buy paddy and rice from local farmers after harvest and sell it when the price increases: on one occasion they earned a profit of INR1,500 in one week. They store the paddy and rice in the community hall which was constructed with Gram Vikas's help. Also, in season, they collect sabai grass and make rope to sell in the nearest market.

The impact of the RHEP in this village has been tremendous. Although the problem of alcoholism still exists, it is reduced to a large extent. People now take an active interest in the local market economy, and have much-raised self-esteem.

---

have the ability and confidence to continue to grow even after their withdrawal, otherwise it is possible that all the positive gains will be completely undermined.

Training in masonry, plumbing and electrics

Gram Vikas points out that often livelihood activities focus on the less vulnerable poor, or the non-vulnerable, who possess a minimum degree of entrepreneurial ability. However the landless people, the bottom 10–25 per cent of the population, who have suffered centuries of exclusion and marginalization, are very low in self-esteem; they feel that they possess no entrepreneurial skills and as a result are not confident to start even a small business. It is also a fact that the poorest of the poor cannot afford to take any risk with their meagre income. There is no room for error: not earning means not having enough food to eat – it is literally a matter of life and death. These people would never apply to receive support for an organized livelihood-generation activity.

Gram Vikas believes that the only effective way to alleviate the poverty and improve the livelihood possibilities of the landless is through skills training. In the early stages of their intervention, before construction of the toilets and bathing rooms begins, young local men and women who are unskilled labourers are trained in basic masonry skills (see Photo 6.1). On completion of the 75-day training course they construct toilets, bathing rooms and overhead water tanks under the supervision of master masons and an engineer. During construction of the RHEP infrastructure a plumber also trains local youths in plumbing, electricity and pump maintenance. The newly trained masons are assured of work with Gram Vikas for up to two years if they want it, until they become skilled and confident enough to take on work orders by themselves. The masons can also get contracts for work in nearby towns – they do not have to depend on Gram Vikas. Masons are always in demand; even in the little towns as soon as people get some money they spend it on improving their house. Gram Vikas also conducts training to upgrade existing masons' skills (for people who have received the basic masonry training and other masons): training in different masonry bonds, stone dressing, steel-fixing (bending reinforcing bars), roof-casting and painting. These master masons supervise the RHEP construction work and lead training in other project areas.

Photo 6.1 Village masons building RHEP infrastructure
Source: Gram Vikas.

Gram Vikas has successfully trained 1,233 new masons in 22 RHEP project areas since November 1999 (in their 27 years of operation it has trained over 6,000 masons). During the year finishing at the end of July 2006 it trained almost 430 masons, of whom 85 were women. Men who could previously not earn even INR30 per day in the non-agricultural season earn INR60–80 per day after being trained as a mason, and INR120–150 per day after about two years. And, as stated earlier, masons are always in demand; an internal study of 281 masons has shown an increase of 50 per cent in the average number of days employed. Mason training has meant that 15 families in Bolangir district alone have not had to migrate for seasonal work. Women's wages are slightly lower and they remain dependent on Gram Vikas to provide them with work, as there is still resistance to employing trained women masons in the mainstream market. This resistance is being overcome by Gram Vikas through the establishment of guilds composed of both men and women to take on building contracts together. Box 6.3 describes one female mason's experience.

Gram Vikas brought the technology for the vertical shaft brick kiln (VSBK) to Orissa (it originated in China). This is a non-mechanized and energy-efficient system of producing quality bricks; it is economically viable and easily used by rural populations. VSBKs are 30 per cent more

---

Box 6.3 Sindhu Majhi: a female mason

Sindhu Majhi is a young girl who has made a mark for herself as a mason. Sindhu's father is no longer able to work and her mother struggled to support their family of five all by herself; they did not have enough land to feed the family. Sindhu worked as a daily labourer to increase her family's income; however, due to poor wages she was still unable to support the family.

In 2003, Gram Vikas organized training in masonry for landless young men and women and Sindhu was one of the participants in this 75-day training course. Her parents and neighbours were opposed to her participation but she completed the training and returned to her village. The villagers criticized her decision to be a mason and her family discouraged her from continuing down that avenue. They said: 'Sindhu, there is women's work and men's work, roles are not interchangeable. So why take up something that you are destined to fail at?'

Sindhu ignored them and helped in the construction of toilets and bathing rooms in the village and worked on other building projects in the area. She now has enough work throughout the year and is able to support her parents and younger siblings. She hopes some day to learn how to cast a roof. Talking on the subject of masonry she says: 'I thought only men could be masons and women cooked nice things for them to eat when they got home – but cooking and masonry work aren't so different after all, both involve putting things together to create something bigger. I now feel a sense of self-worth and am more self-confident – I earn a respectable livelihood.' On the subject of her marriage she says: 'I will not marry out of necessity because I now know I am able to support myself.'

efficient than the commonly found brick kilns and 50 per cent more efficient than small local clamps. Though brick-making is generally a seasonal activity, the VSBK enables the firing of bricks throughout the year, providing stable employment and income. VSBKs have been effective in reducing the yearly migration among brick moulders. A VSBK provides regular employment to 30 people for a minimum of 250 days per year, with kiln workers receiving INR60–70 per day. In addition about 30 families of green-brick moulders can each earn up to around INR10,000 per year.[25] The village corpus fund can be used as collateral for loans to build these VSBK enterprises. Gram Vikas operates two kilns directly and has supported the setting-up of two kilns owned and managed by village communities, and four private kilns.

Community forestry, fish farming and horticulture

Gram Vikas motivates communities to collectively manage their existing social forestry plantations and fish ponds; community land is leased for paddy (rice) growing. These activities increase a community's income; co-management and sharing of benefits boosts the sense of unity in the community, and managing the forests means that they are protected for future generations rather than degraded. People are encouraged to regenerate common and private wastelands by growing trees for fuel, fruit, fodder and timber, and also by developing small horticulture plantations.

Women from Tamana have developed 15 acres of horticulture patches on an individual ownership basis, growing species such as mango, guava, custard apple and jackfruit. At least 25 per cent of the total yield from these horticulture patches goes to the village fund which, among other things, is used to meet O&M costs of the water supply. The ownership of the patches remains in the women's names. This represents a break with tradition, since previously all deeds would have been in men's names, and is an indication of the empowerment of these women.

Overgrown village ponds are cleaned up for scientific fish farming, with varieties of fish that produce good income. Ponds that used to yield an income of INR5,000 annually now yield INR40,000. Fish farming is traditionally a men's domain, but in some villages women's SHGs have leased a pond and carry out fish farming as a business. In Ganjam district a total of 43 acres of ponds are now farmed and in the year to March 2006 these ponds yielded a profit of INR206,250.

In tribal areas where villagers traditionally practise *bogodo* (slash-and-burn cultivation) people are shown how to develop cultivable land by levelling it, digging farm ponds and constructing bunds. Appropriate plantations are established according to the soil conditions, but special priority is given to cashew trees because of their high market value. Cultivation of pineapple, lemon, orange, mango, jackfruit, paddy and vegetables are also promoted. Improved agriculture and horticulture has meant a significant increase in income and reduced dependence on *bogodo* for many villagers.

Health and hygiene

As part of their RHEP intervention Gram Vikas educates people about health and hygiene matters: hand-washing, nail-cutting, clothes washing, hair-cutting and the importance of cleanliness in general are covered. Women in SHGs and children at school are especially targeted for this training; it is hoped that by catching children at a young age hygienic habits will become second nature and they will also enforce the message at home (see Photo 6.2).

Gram Vikas encourages and facilitates villagers to access government primary-health services for basic medicines, immunization of eligible children, and ante-natal and post-natal care of mothers. In remote areas that do not have government services Gram Vikas also runs dispensaries from their project offices, with trained health staff to provide essential medical facilities. Efforts are made to detect and treat incidences of malaria, leprosy and TB in a timely fashion. Malaria, for instance, is endemic in many of Gram Vikas's working areas and the disease has caused illness and death among their workers. Households are made aware of the government's provision of mosquito nets and malaria curative medication. SDC found in their assessment (2000) that villagers in Samantrapur were 'well aware that the provision of better drainage in all parts of the village for sullage (wastewater) and rainwater is crucial to prevent the breeding of mosquitoes, and related diseases'.

Box 6.4 Uttami Pradhan: an enterprising woman

Uttami Pradhan has three children and an alcoholic husband. She was illiterate and her family had no regular source of income, not even agricultural land. In April 1999 she applied for and got a loan of INR3,670 from Gram Vikas. With this money, she opened a shop in the village to sell various items of daily use like soaps, matchboxes, washing powder, spices, bread, biscuits, eggs, paan, some snacks and tea. This was the start to improving her life.

Now her daily turnover is around INR300 of which a third comes from selling tea. With this source of regular income, by mid-2000 she had already repaid 90 per cent of her loan. She had also bought 600 sq ft of land and deposited INR1,500 to construct a *pucca* house. Her children regularly go to school. With this shop Uttami's village, Kinchling, has become a centre of many activities in the area, and others have opened similar shops in nearby villages.

Inspired by her success, Uttami's husband asked Gram Vikas to assist him in buying a bicycle to collect wood and other forestry produce which he would then sell in nearby areas. With a loan of INR1,400 he bought the bicycle with a precondition of repaying INR20 per day from his income. Uttami's family is well on its way to economic stability.

Plate 6.2 The importance of hygiene is emphasized at school
Source: Gram Vikas.

Protecting the water supply and managing waste disposal are essential in preventing diseases and reducing morbidity and mortality rates in the future. Reducing the incidence of disease has the knock-on effect of reducing the government's spending on high health-care costs. Data on crude birth and death rates, the incidence of diseases and nutrition aspects, especially in relation to young children, can help in evaluating the impacts of the RHEP's health component. Improvements in health are likely to lead to a reduction in household health expenditure and a reduction in workdays lost due to illness, so monitoring health improvements is also one of the best ways of estimating the positive effects of the RHEP on poverty reduction.[26]

Data for the year ended 31 March 2006 show that of 81,000 RHEP villagers in six districts the majority of people were free from diseases during the year (see Table 6.2). Only 1 per cent suffered diarrhoea that required treatment and 0.2 per cent were treated for scabies. Fever and colds were the main illnesses, suffered by 4–6 per cent of people. Malaria affected 3 per cent of the population. An internal analysis by Gram Vikas of their health data for a sample of 4,976 people shows an 85 per cent reduction in illnesses overall after implementation of the RHEP, with an 88–90 per cent reduction in incidence of diarrhoea, jaundice and malaria (see Table 6.3).

Periodic growth monitoring of children is carried out in RHEP villages to detect malnutrition. In an effort to help improve nutrition villagers

Table 6.2 Illnesses treated in the year to 31 March 2006

Illness	Scabies	Diarrhoea	Dysentery	Typhoid	Jaundice	Fever	Cold and cough	TB	Malaria
No. of patients treated	189	859	0	71	103	4,741	2,914	11	2105
% of illnesses	1.7	7.8	0	0.6	0.9	43.1	26.5	0.1	19.1
% of pop.	0.2	1	0	0.1	0.1	6	4	0	3

Source: Author, based on data compiled by Gram Vikas for the Annual Report 2005–6 (Gram Vikas, 2006).
Note: These figures relate to 81,000 RHEP villagers in six districts: Ganjam, Bolangir, Bargarh, Keonjhar, Nayagarh and Kalahandi.

Table 6.3 Reduction in incidence of illness after implementing the RHEP

	Diarrhoea	Typhoid	Jaundice	Fever	Malaria	Other	Total
No. of patients treated per year before RHEP (A)	321	11	31	1,185	951	285	2,784
% of illness by disease	11.5	0.4	1.1	42.6	34.2	10.2	
% of population	6.5	0.2	0.6	23.8	19.1	5.7	
No. of patients treated per year after RHEP (B)	37	9	3	231	112	17	408
% of illness by disease	9.1	2.2	0.7	56.6	27.4	4.0	
% of population	0.7	0.2	0.1	4.6	2.2	0.3	
% reduction in illness (A–B)/A	88	18	90	81	88	94	85

Source: Gram Vikas.
Note: These figures relate to 11 villages (population 4,976) which implemented the RHEP during the period 1995–2002.

are encouraged to grow kitchen vegetable gardens, using the wastewater from the bathing rooms; and the fruits from trees that are planted near the latrine soak pits supplement this. In Mayurbhanj district 20 SHGs are running midday meal programmes in schools to ensure that children get properly fed. Gram Vikas report that since their intervention fewer than 5 per cent of children are now malnourished. Unfortunately baseline data were not available for comparison with pre-intervention days, but the GoI in its 10th Five-Year Plan states that more than 50 per cent of the children under the age of five years in India are moderately or severely malnourished (GoI, 2002a: 18).[27] It would seem that Gram Vikas has effected a considerable improvement in this health indicator.

Data from Gram Vikas's RHEP villages show that infant mortality was 40 per 1,000 live births in Ganjam district for the year ended 31 March 2006 (see Table 6.4), and mortality of 2–5 year olds was 21 per 1,000 live births, giving an under-five mortality of 61 per 1,000 live births. UNICEF quote the under-five mortality rate in India at 85 per 1,000 live births in 2004 (UNICEF, 2006).[24] In their 10th Five-Year Plan the GoI states that it aims to bring down the infant mortality rate to less than 60 per 1,000 and the child mortality rate to below 10 per 1,000 (GoI, 2002a: 21). Gram Vikas has already achieved that target for the infant mortality rate.

Most under-fives in Ganjam district RHEP villages died of 'other' causes, such as accidents (15 in total, 58 per cent of all under-five deaths); malaria was the next biggest killer (31 per cent), with diarrhoea accounting for 8 per cent of under-fives' deaths. No infants died of diarrhoea or jaundice during the year.[29] Gunyon gives a figure of 28 per cent for child deaths due to diarrhoea and dehydration in India (Gunyon, 1998: 5). Improvements in health, and particularly reduction of child deaths due to waterborne diseases, seem to indicate that people in RHEP villages in Ganjam district have taken on board the health–hygiene link and are following improved hygienic practices. This is backed up by the fact that toilets inspected by the author were spotless and showed evidence of being in regular use, and village streets were swept clean.

Gram Vikas has created widespread awareness among communities that it is their right to receive regular visits from health-care workers. The communities have become active in seeking out local auxiliary nurses and midwives (ANMs) and demanding the services to which they are entitled. In the past couple of years Gram Vikas has also encouraged villagers to subscribe to the *Janashree Bima Yojana* (JBY) of the Life

Table 6.4 Mortality rates and causes in Ganjam district RHEP villages

Age	Malaria/ fever	Diarrhoea	Jaundice	Heart disease	TB	Old age	Other	Total
<1 yr	5	0	0	1	0	-	11	17
2–5 yrs	3	2	0	0	0	-	4	9
6–18 yrs	5	0	0	0	0	-	2	7
>18 yrs	2	0	3	13	2	97	3	120
Total	15	2	3	14	2	97	20	153
Infant and child mortality rates (deaths per 1,000 live births)								
<1 yr	12	0	0	2	0	-	26	40
2–5 yrs	7	5	0	0	0	-	9	21

Source: Author, compiled from Gram Vikas's unpublished data for year to 31 March 2006.
Note: There were 424 live births in RHEP villages in Ganjam district during the year.

Insurance Corporation (LIC) of India, an insurance scheme for the benefit of the masses. An annual premium of INR100 provides insurance cover of INR20,000 in case of natural death and INR50,000 in case of accident. An accompanying scheme of the JBY is the *Shikshya Sahayak Yojana* (SSY, Education Assistance Scheme), which provides scholarships to an insured persons' children who are studying in classes 9–12; 59 children are currently receiving INR100 per month under the SSY scheme.

Education

Access to education for all eligible children is one of Gram Vikas's central aims. To ensure all children receive primary education, Gram Vikas delivers awareness on the importance of education to communities that have little, if any, history of education. Freeing up girl children from water-carrying means that they can go to school and in the evenings the mother, who is also free from carrying water, will have more time to look after the smaller children, thus making it easier for the girls to have study time. Village committees, with support from Gram Vikas staff, ensure existing government schools function fully and all eligible boys and girls enrol. Gram Vikas assists the village committee in applying for the schools sanitation grant described on p. 24. As stated earlier, children at school are especially targeted for hygiene training. Gram Vikas encourages government school teachers to participate in development activities and training programmes in the villages through events such as school-based sanitation workshops.

In the year to 31 March 2006, 95 per cent of eligible boys from RHEP villages in Ganjam district, and 94 per cent of eligible girls, were enrolled in school. Gram Vikas says that attendance rates for boys and girls are well above 80 per cent. Attendance figures for village schools in Ganjam district for the year to 31 March 2006 (see Table 6.5) show that 66 per cent of pupils attended school for more than 20 days; 8 per cent of boys and 9 per cent of girls dropped out from school. Generally speaking,

Table 6.5 Enrolment and attendance in village schools in Ganjam district

	Boys	Girls	Total	
Enrolled	2,710	2,559	5,269	
Dropouts	221	227		
% dropouts	8	9		
Attendance	>20 days	10–19 days	<10 days	0 days
No. of pupils	3,478	1,317	316	158
% of total	66	25	6	3

Source: Author, compiled from Gram Vikas's unpublished data for year to 31 March 2006.

pupils drop out from school because the family has to migrate in search of work.

Gram Vikas puts special emphasis on motivating dropouts, and those who have low attendance rates or failed exams, to re-enrol. Intensive one-month courses are organized to reintegrate these students into the education system, raise their standards and promote them to the next class. In villages where there is demand, adult literacy classes are held.

Gram Vikas's Phase 1 baseline survey found many reasons for children not attending school (Gram Vikas, 2003b). Some children had to provide supplementary income for their families and so could not attend school; in other cases inadequate school infrastructure or the unreliability of teachers were main contributing factors. It has been shown already that Gram Vikas takes steps to improve people's livelihoods; this hopefully also has the effect of freeing children so that they can attend school.

There is a shortage of trained teachers in Orissa; there may be up to 100 children per teacher. In 118 RHEP villages, where the teachers were not attending schools regularly, Gram Vikas has encouraged villagers to employ someone from the vicinity to run special classes for the children. Groups of around 10 children pay approximately INR150 per month between them for 1–1.5 hours' tuition per day. Communities pay as much as INR1,100–2,000 per month for such services. This highlights the fact that people now feel education is important; if it is not made available by government communities will take steps to arrange it for themselves. (See Box 6.5)

As part of their education children are introduced to the concept of saving, and children's saving groups are set up. The children get about INR2–10 from their parents to lodge in the fund monthly. Once they complete their primary schooling pupils may have to travel a few miles to school and their savings will help to buy a bicycle; or the money may help the parents out in some other way at that time.

Villagers' perceptions of the RHEP

'Our village is better than the town. We have 24*7 [continuous, 24 hours, seven days a week] piped water supply to all families, without exception. Every family has their own toilet and bathing room as well. When we seek marriage alliances, our daughters ask us would there be similar facilities there as well,' says Lalita Malik of Tamana village. This appears to be a resounding 'yes' for the RHEP from Tamana. Similar comments were made by people in other villages during group discussions aimed at finding out their views on the RHEP.[30] One of the women in Neeladripur said: 'If [my daughter] was going to get married into a village that had no running water and no bathrooms and toilets first the village would have to implement RHEP and then we'll consider it.' That

Box 6.5 Changing attitudes to education in Kusagumma

Kusagumma is a village of small farmers in Ganjam district. Education was never important for the people; in fact to them it was a waste of time and energy. But when the RHEP was implemented in 2000 the villagers underwent some changes in attitude: they decided to appoint a tutor for 60 school-going children because the government school did not function effectively.

The children say they study because it makes one clever. They learn how to calculate and keep accounts; some want to write letters, some to read the newspaper and many want to go out to work. Because of a lack of role models, the children have very humble ambitions. Most of the boys want to set up shops or work in Surat (in faraway Gujarat state on the west coast), and most girls want to stay at home, just as they see their mothers do. Some girls quip that they want to be engineers and doctors, and then laugh with embarrassment at the perceived impossibility of their dream. Most girls will be taken out of school after 9th or 10th grade, to be married off or because of financial constraints.

The children in Kusagumma have three savings groups; they save INR5 every month out of their pocket money. Each group has a president and a secretary (chosen by consensus) who organize monthly meetings and manage records. If there are any disagreements the children negotiate to settle differences. They say that they save because it is a good habit: that they can help their parents in times of need, they can use the money for their own education and of course can extend credit to people. They seem sure they do not mind sacrificing some goodies to save up. As an organized children's group they also supervise personal hygiene, check that toilets are kept clean, and undertake to keep their streets and surroundings clean.

same woman also said that the women try to avoid going to villages that do not have toilets, so she does not go to visit her mother, instead she gets her mother to visit her.

Constraints against joining the RHEP

A variety of reasons have been given by villagers for not wanting to join the RHEP. Borrowing from an analysis method used by Noor and Ashrafee (2004), the reasons can be broadly gathered under the following themes: pipe-dream (only rich people in cities have 24-hour running water and toilets), distrust (the NGO might run away with their money), disharmony (village too divided; people will not work together), toilet (do not want one; all castes get the same design), landless, cost (corpus fund; government scheme gives free toilets).

The pipe-dream theme was a very strong constraint in the earlier RHEP villages. Gram Vikas had great difficulty in getting five pilot villages to agree to implement the RHEP and had preliminary talks with at least 500 villages at that stage. Villagers knew that the state government could not provide 24-hour running water even for its own officials' residences, so they could not imagine how a small organization like Gram Vikas could possibly provide them with 24-hour running water. In fact this pipe-dream constraint was not only a barrier to villagers: national and international agencies (Gram Vikas's donors) and government officials did not believe that a small NGO in Orissa would be able to provide 24-hour running water – everyone had doubts that it would work. However, once the RHEP was successfully implemented in the pilot villages they were used as showcases for government, donors and other villages to prove that it could be done. The pipe-dream theme is no longer a constraint to implementation.

Another constraint raised in the earlier RHEP villages was the distrust theme. The sorts of things mentioned under this theme are: 'what if leaders and government officials siphon away all the [corpus fund] money'; 'what if we lose all the village wealth'; 'they [Gram Vikas] must want something in return for the [subsidy] money'. Gram Vikas got around these constraints by having the villagers themselves collect and control the finances through the elected VEC. The five pilot villages had understanding leaders who had worked with Gram Vikas in the biogas project and trusted them to complete the job, but without that initial trust it is unlikely that the RHEP would ever have got off the ground. This theme is no longer a constraint once people talk to villagers who have experienced working with Gram Vikas and the RHEP; Gram Vikas initially paid the cost of these exposure trips for villagers.

Disharmony within communities has always been, and continues to be, a major constraint to joining the RHEP. Getting 100 per cent consensus is very difficult where people have different political affiliations, are divided between the different leaders who play a role in the village affairs and distrust each other. Because the basis for the RHEP is to use water and sanitation as a means to changing people's lives by getting all members of a community cooperating, Gram Vikas will not implement the programme until everyone agrees. It can take more than a year to convince everyone. The people of Neeladripur said that one of the biggest difficulties they faced was working together. Neeladripur is very divided along both caste lines and political lines, but the village has three very strong leaders, one of whom dedicated his time for a year solely to getting people in the village to work together for the RHEP.

Having to build a toilet is a constraint to many villagers; the men in particular are comfortable with their practice of open defecation, so why should they change? Most villagers only want the water, not the toilets, but when they realize that they cannot get water without a toilet they reconsider. Reasons given for not wanting a toilet include: 'our forefathers shat under the open sky – diseases don't spread that way', and 'I find it so restricting to sit in a box'. Health education goes some way to increasing demand for toilets, but until villagers –

particularly men – actually start using toilets they are not really convinced of the need.[31]

Lack of choice in toilet and bathing room design is not generally a constraint to joining the RHEP; a toilet is usually a luxury to everyone in a village. However, in some GC villages, where some of the better-off higher-caste people would not like to see their servant have the same facilities as they have, a lack of choice can be a constraint. For this reason wealthier families can opt to pay for a slightly more costly toilet if they choose, but it is not actively encouraged by Gram Vikas because poorer families tend to want to 'keep up with the Jones'.[32]

Being landless is a constraint only in the very early stages of intervention by Gram Vikas. Before the Agreement is signed Gram Vikas facilitates the village community in identifying some land belonging to the community, or the government, on which landless people can build toilets and bathing rooms. In this instance the land is not legally signed over to the family in question, but there is no fear of repossession: once government land is being used by a village it cannot be repossessed by the government, and community land legally must always be owned by the community. In some instances the better-off donate or sell land to the landless, who are not always poor but just may not have enough space around their house for building. In this case a legally binding contract is drawn up. The acquired land must be within 20 m of the landless family's house so that the family can have its own private latrine, just like all other families. This is a big difference between Gram Vikas's approach and that of the VERC's TSC: there are no shared toilets, each family has its own, good-quality toilet.

The corpus fund is a big constraint to poor villagers and affording it seemed an impossibility for some in Samiapalli. Gram Vikas assists villagers in coming up with innovative solutions to this constraint, like using community property to generate income. (See pp. 98–100 for some examples of how the corpus fund is generated by villagers.)

The two constraints of being landless or not being able to afford the corpus fund are sometimes overcome through the generosity of better-off households. There may be a couple of motives behind better-off people subsidizing poor people in order to implement the RHEP. Take the following scenario: I'm a wealthy man and I don't have a running water system. One motive for my subsidizing others is that it saves me money in the long run. If I want to set up my own running-water system I have to dig my own well, build a water tank, buy a pump and maintain the whole system from my own pocket. Under the RHEP I can get a running-water system where all the costs are shared by everybody in the village – it is much cheaper! A second motive is improved health. Even if I build my own toilet, if people persist in open defecation the water will continue to be polluted; food will continue to be contaminated and my family's, and the whole village's, health will continue to be affected. So it is in my interest – and indeed the whole village's interest – that every household has and uses a toilet. (This factor is what drives better-off households to donate land for toilets and bathing rooms.)

One other constraint to getting the RHEP implemented, as mentioned by one of Gram Vikas's project coordinators, was the fact that the government TSC provides free toilets to BPL households. Because corrupt village leaders can get a cut from the TSC scheme, they urge the villagers to take the TSC toilets (these leaders can get no cut from the RHEP).

Drivers for joining the RHEP

This section will look at the drivers for sanitation mentioned by RHEP villagers. When talking about drivers for adopting sanitation, it must be realized that women are the ones who are most interested in sanitation at the outset; men tend to see the benefits only at a later stage, as illustrated by a comment from Tamana's headman (see endnote 27). The issue of toilets did not seem to matter to men; they could live without them, and without running water too.

A variety of reasons were given for wanting to join the RHEP. Using a similar analysis method to that used by Noor and Ashrafee (2004), the reasons can be broadly gathered under the following themes: practical (time-saving), privacy (saving embarrassment), health (diseases, safety), prestige and social pressure (if they do not agree no one gets water, villages already under RHEP teasing them, poor marriage prospects). See Table 6.6 to compare the drivers found for the RHEP with those found for other sanitation projects.

The one thing that first pushed all women to join the RHEP was the prospect of running water: they all wanted water. In some villages women have to walk 1–1.5 km for water, taking between two and three hours to collect water for the whole family. In the rainy season this chore is even more arduous when tracks become muddy and slippery.

Privacy while defecating was another very strong driver for women. In Neeladripur the women wanted toilets because that area is very flat, open farmland with nowhere to hide when defecating in the open: in the rainy season it is too muddy and slippery to go far. A woman in Tamana also said that the main reason she wanted a toilet was to save herself the embarrassment of going out like a thief to defecate in the open. It seems that a lot of leverage could be gained from emphasizing this dignity issue. In Orissa, as in many conservative societies, a woman's integrity is paramount. It should be possible to work on men and urge them to adopt sanitation by playing on this: asking them how they can allow their women to defecate in public, such a shameful practice.

Social pressure can be an effective driving force in getting people to join the RHEP. Tamana villagers found that when the majority of the village was in accord the rest over time realized that if they continued to disagree then no one would get water, so they agreed to join up. In another village women were being teased and humiliated by the women from the neighbouring village where the RHEP had already been implemented: 'You women, you have no shame'. This humiliation made the women determined to make their men agree to join the RHEP. (The story of Mohakhand is related in Box 4.1.)

Safety was quoted by some men and women as a reason for wanting toilets (Gram Vikas, 2003a); there is a real danger of being bitten by snakes or attacked by bears when going out at night. There is probably also a risk to women and girls of being molested or raped.

Tamana's headman said that another thing that convinced them to join the RHEP was talk about health: 'We had a lot of bad health, we used to get a lot of scabies and a lot of diarrhoea and dysentery because where we shat we had a bath in the same place.' He said that learning about the link between sanitary practices and improved health convinced

Table 6.6 Motivational factors for sanitation demand

Factor	Bangladesh TSC	Tamil Nadu	Kenya	Benin	Orissa RHEP
Prestige and social pressure	✓ (c, w, v)		✓ (c, w)	✓ (m)	✓ (w, m)
External (expatriate visitors)	✓ (v)			✓ (m)	
Practical (time and money saving)	✓ (w, v, c)	✓			✓ (w)
Process (goo calculation,[1] slogans)	✓ (c, v)				
Privacy for women (purdah)	✓ (w, v)			✓	
Privacy for women (indignity)	✓ (w)	✓			✓ (w)
Health (safety)	✓ (v, w, c)			✓	✓ (w, m)
Health (diseases)	✓ (v, w, c)		✓ (c, m, w, e)	✓ (m)	✓ (m)
Aesthetic	✓ (w, v)			✓	
Little space for open defecation[2]		✓	✓ (w, c, m, e)	✓	
Convenience			✓ (w)	✓	✓ (w)
Ease restricted mobility				✓	

Source: Author, compiled from Noor and Ashrafee (2004), Gunyon (1998), Jackson (2004), Jenkins and Curtis (2005), and this Keirns (2006).

[1]'Goo calculation' refers to a participatory process whereby the community calculates the faeces contribution per household – it is an awareness raising tool that helps communities to realize the magnitude and extent of the problem.

[2]Less bush available for open defecation due to more land being cultivated.

Notes: i) Factors are listed in the order of significance found in Noor and Ashrafee's (2004) study of TSC Bangladesh; ii) c, w, v, m refer to children, women, villager and men groups respectively (only the first three types of groups were surveyed in Bangladesh); iii) bold lettering indicates groups that mentioned a factor frequently; ordinary text indicates 'sometimes mentioned'.

them of the need for toilets and bathing rooms. However, judging by the facts that this very man said he had not wanted a toilet in the beginning, and that health was not mentioned as a driver by any other villagers, the author suspects that the headman was convinced after the fact that health was a good reason for sanitation.

Implemented RHEP acts as a driver for another village

Gram Vikas says that there is now a pull factor in the expansion of the programme, whereas before recent years it was almost all push, trying to convince people to join up. 'About two years ago people started coming and not just enquiring but wanting RHEP. It depends on the area as to whether men, women, tribals or a particular caste come to us. In some areas if there are lots of villages close by that have RHEP then women come; in other areas if the men have heard about RHEP then the men come.' (Gram Vikas, 2006a.) For Neeladripur villagers, their neighbours had already implemented the RHEP about two years earlier; it is very likely that this demonstration effect was a pull factor.

Several people (men and women) from different RHEP villages have stated that they would not marry their daughters into villages that did not have running water and toilets. This social demand factor – people looking for improved marriage prospects rather than the direct benefit of improved health – may be a driver behind the growing number of villages that are approaching Gram Vikas for assistance. It is certainly a selling point that is worth exploring.

Another driver is the snob factor. If a villager sees someone he (or she) considers to be a lower-caste person with running water and a toilet and bathing room his pride will not let him bear the indignity of not having at least equal facilities. This driver urged the people of the Oriya village, beside Tamana, to implement the RHEP; and it is the factor that Gram Vikas expects will drive any dissenting better-off higher-caste people in a village to finally join the RHEP.

Money saving was mentioned as a reason for joining the RHEP, as were the forming of SHGs and access to loans. Financial drivers are not immediately obvious, because the programme has considerable upfront costs; however, the reduction in medical expenses due to better health and the instilling of a savings and budgeting ethos which leads to more disposable income could be strong drivers if they were pushed as benefits by other villages.

Benefits resulting from the RHEP

Villagers mentioned many benefits that they had experienced as a result of the RHEP. These can be grouped into general themes: improvement of women's lot (time saving, dignity, reduced gynaecological problems, increased confidence), general health, financial (reduced medical bills, saving and budgeting), village improvements (cleaner environment, education) and social harmony.

Tamana's headman said that there had been a lot of development for the women especially. Women had had to suffer the indignity and danger of defecating in the open; they endured a lot of diseases because they had to bathe in dirty water and with their saris on, so medical expenses were high. Toilets and bathing rooms have made a huge improvement to women's lives, since now women can bathe in the privacy of their own room and those medical bills are essentially gone. Women also have more free time now since they do not need to spend hours carrying water.

The women of Neeladripur said that before Gram Vikas started working with them 'we wouldn't leave the house or sit in a room with the men, but now we can'. Not only that, they are more than willing to voice opinions in the presence of men. Gram Vikas helped the women to form SHGs and showed them how to deposit money in the bank. Now the women bring the men to the bank and teach them how to fill in the slips. The confidence of the Neeladripur women in group discussion was remarkable. Looking at them exchanging views and joking with men it was hard to believe that just one year before these women would not even have sat in a group like this.

All villagers said that general health had improved immensely. Where before people in Tamana suffered 'a lot' from scabies and diarrhoea, now they suffer 'just normal fevers, colds, things like that', meaning much reduced medical bills. Villagers had difficulty in quantifying how much the medical bills had dropped; in Neeladripur they said that more than 10 per cent of the population had always had scabies, but they no longer suffer from that disease because they have plentiful water. The day that the group discussion was held in Neeladripur was the 'first day in a long time' that someone went to the hospital with diarrhoea. The general feeling was: 'I know I have gone to the doctor a lot less'.

Having implemented the RHEP, villagers gain confidence in their ability such that they are able to carry out projects to improve the village infrastructure. When Gram Vikas first went to Samiapalli the village was very dirty – 'you could hardly walk one or two feet without stepping in faeces' (Gram Vikas, 2006a) – now it is spotless. Both Samiapalli and Tamana have asked for and received funding for concrete roads from visiting state government politicians, and the villagers build the roads themselves. In Samiapalli less than 50 per cent of children were going to school; now nearly all go up to 5th standard.

Regarding financial benefits resulting from the programme, Tamana's headman made the point that before Gram Vikas worked with them they had no concept of saving, that any money they had was immediately spent. A similar scenario ruled in Samiapalli. Both of these older villages had serious problems with alcohol abuse. Now both villages have strong community funds and are highly successful models of the RHEP.

During the group discussions it was obvious that the thing that most surprised people was that the whole village actually succeeded in working together towards an aim. Even in Tamana, a wholly tribal village, the headman did not expect that they could all come together and pitch in to make the RHEP happen. He thought the whole village would never agree on anything. Any previous projects that had been implemented only required the men or the women of the village to come together for a short time – for a cause that ended – so they did not have to stay unified. No other project included all the men and all the women.

Comments along these lines by villagers highlight the importance of Gram Vikas's insistence on 100 per cent involvement in the RHEP by the headmen and headwomen of all families in order to build community spirit. When that spirit is ignited there seems to be no end to the desire of the people to find a way to help themselves.

The RHEP approach: success or failure?

'Very few programmes have reached more than 100,000 people. And even when latrines have been constructed, many are not used or not used as latrines.' (WELL, 2006)

The RHEP is undoubtedly a success as regards improving water and sanitation for villagers. As a direct result of the programme over 150,000 people now have uninterrupted running water piped to the house, on-site sanitation, and clean environments. After RHEP implementation there has been a significant improvement in all vulnerability indicators (malnutrition in children, number of cases of diarrhoea reported to clinics, proximity to safe water supply, use of safe sanitation methods and access to clinical services). This suggests that people's vulnerability, one aspect of poverty, has decreased. But the RHEP is not just about water and sanitation; it is about 100 per cent inclusion, gender equity, social equity and justice, self-esteem and dignity. The RHEP is a clear example of an integrated and holistic approach to development.

A preliminary internal cost-benefit analysis conducted by Gram Vikas has shown that the benefits resulting from the programme are more than twice as large as the costs incurred, in some villages more than three times as large (de Wit, 2005). On the cost side of the equation, Gram Vikas's administration costs were the most important. This is not surprising, because the motivational aspect of the RHEP costs the field staff a lot of time, and more field staff means more administration. The second most important cost is the construction cost, most of it for building the toilets and bathing rooms for every household.

CHAPTER 7
Financing Gram Vikas's water and sanitation programme

This chapter looks at the cost per household of implementing the RHEP. A breakdown is given for contributions made by householders themselves (and how they deal with it), funding received through GoI schemes and the support given by donors (national and international).

Project implementation costs

As at December 2006, the total cost of constructing a toilet and bathing room under the RHEP was around INR8,500, as shown in Table 7.1. Gram Vikas's subsidy of INR3,000 per household amounts to around 35 per cent of that. The remaining costs are borne by the people themselves (corpus fund INR1,000, labour and local materials worth around INR4,500). For BPL households part of the cost, INR1,200, is financed by the GoI under the Total Sanitation Campaign. Thus the total support extended to BPL families is significantly higher than to above-poverty-line (APL) households; BPL households pay around 50 per cent of the toilet and bathing room capital cost.

The water supply system (comprising of an overhead tank, distribution pipelines and three taps to each household) is constructed with support from the GoI under their *Swajaldhara* rural water-supply scheme. *Swajaldhara* proposes a 90–10 partnership with people (with the people contributing 10 per cent of the cost of construction). However, the water tanks constructed under Gram Vikas's RHEP exceed the government provisions by more than three times (storage capacity of only 10 litres per head is provided under *Swajaldhara*, if allowed for at all, as explained on p. 20). The community must make up the difference in costs that result from providing the increased storage capacity. Gram Vikas has

Table 7.1 Typical costs (in INR) of the RHEP per household as at December 2006

Particulars	Cost	Household funds		External funds	
Toilets and bathing rooms	8,500	5,500	65%	3,000	35%
Water supply systems	9,000	2,250	25%	6,750	75%
Institutional and software costs	4,250	—	—	4,250	100%
Total	21,750	7,750	36%	14,000	64%

Source: Gram Vikas.

been able to motivate communities to make up for the deficit in all cases to date. Hence, villagers contribute usually up to 25–30 per cent of the total capital costs of their water supply. In a typical village of 50 households, villagers contribute around INR2,250 per household. In larger villages the actual cost per household will be less because of economies of scale, and in smaller villages the actual cost per household will be greater.

Gram Vikas estimates that the software costs of project implementation are around 25 per cent of the construction and material costs of a toilet and bathing room, that is, INR2,125. Software includes the costs incurred by Gram Vikas on capacity-building of the community over a period of between three and five years: developing leadership qualities (especially among weaker sections of the community), building gender equity, engaging with the *panchayat*, ensuring the availability of good-quality health and education services and enhancing livelihood opportunities through skill training.

Institutional costs (all administrative overheads and staff costs) incurred on the programme by Gram Vikas have been estimated to also be around 25 per cent of the construction and material costs of a toilet and bathing room.

All software and programme implementation (institutional) costs are funded solely through Gram Vikas's foreign donors (see p. 101).

The total cost for the whole RHEP intervention in water and sanitation in a village of 50 households is around INR21,750 per household, 36 per cent of which is funded by the beneficiaries.

Contributions by beneficiaries

Data from Gram Vikas's Phase 1 Household Survey (Gram Vikas, 2003b) indicate that in the surveyed households the difference between household income and expenditure was quite small, with an excess of only INR336 per month on average. Implementing the RHEP is certainly a challenge at least to some households; but a preliminary internal cost-benefit analysis conducted by Gram Vikas (de Wit, 2005) has shown that the benefits to villagers resulting from time saved in fetching water, and to a lesser extent reduced health expenditure and reduced loss in earnings due to illness, far outweigh the costs incurred by them. Social benefits such as a better environment, an improved community spirit and increased self-confidence were also found to be significant for villagers.

There are three distinct periods of funding required by villagers implementing the RHEP: the upfront corpus fund contribution (described on pp. 34–5), materials and labour during the building phase and ongoing O&M costs of the water supply.

Different villages have found different ways of coming up with the corpus fund. Gram Vikas can assist with ideas on how to generate the fund, and it can act as guarantor against bank loans, but it does not get involved in actually collecting the money. In Samiapalli the villagers collectively borrowed money against the next crop of cashew nuts from their social forestry plantation. Gram Vikas's project co-ordinator explained that at that time there was a loan scheme with a differential rate of interest for the poorest of the poor, whereby they paid an interest rate of 4 per cent. Samiapalli villagers took an INR100,000 loan against their future crop; they then deposited that money as their corpus fund in an account which earned interest at 13 per cent.

In Tamana people contributed some percentage of their own meagre crops; the village also had a social forestry scheme and they put proceeds from that into their corpus fund. Neeladripur village was a little better-off so some people gave their own money and the remainder of the corpus fund contribution was taken from the existing community fund. In at least one village, utensils, gold and silver were taken as contributions (Gram Vikas, 2003a), while in another village some people paid INR500 in cash and gave labour worth the balance. In this instance Gram Vikas put part of that family's subsidy towards the corpus fund and the family received less subsidy later on. In some villages wealthier people gave up their subsidy entitlement so that it was put against the corpus fund contribution of three or four poorer families; in the west of Orissa a village leader paid the corpus fund charge for 19 more families, giving INR20,000 in total to the corpus fund.

In the pilot phase of the RHEP (1992–5) Gram Vikas paid for all building materials; the villagers only had to collect stone and contribute their labour and to the corpus fund. Since about 1995 some of the cost of materials (or the materials themselves, for example mud, stone, sand, bricks, water, cement) has to be provided by the villagers. Some villages have suitable resources available locally for only the cost of labour to gather it, others use individual contributions or community funds. The people of Tamana paid for materials out of income from their community plantation.

All villagers must contribute labour – such as digging foundations, laying stones, mixing cement, making bricks if suitable materials are freely available – or else pay someone to do the work for them. Both women and men do the labouring. Many poor villagers in Orissa are daily-wage labourers, only being paid for the hours that they work: during the building phase of the RHEP their earning potential is reduced and this could have an effect on their daily household budget. People in Tamana and Neeladripur got around this problem by working longer hours.

The Tamana villagers were happy to give their time – at least in hindsight: 'We still made sure we went and worked in our fields – we got up two hours earlier and we worked into the night, and instead of resting in the afternoon we worked. Gram Vikas was willing to work with our time, so they sent whoever needed to be sent in the evenings or before five o'clock in the mornings. Of course we were exhausted and at times it didn't go so well and we couldn't finish our work in the fields, but the RHEP was for our benefit so it is only right that we should work for it.'

In Samiapalli one family member went out to work and one stayed to labour for the masons. The villagers said they did not have the same amount of money, but they were getting something that was for their benefit and would last a long time. Prior to the RHEP not everyone went out to work regularly – 'sometimes they were just drunk' (Gram Vikas, 2006a) – so this requirement to labour made at least one person in the family go to work every day.

It seems that villagers were happy to work for something that was going to be to their benefit. They were willing to work longer hours so as not to lose other earnings. In some cases wealthier people gave money instead of labour, paying poorer people to do the work for them; it is possible that this created employment for people who would otherwise not have been working.

To ensure the sustainability of the water system villagers must also pay for O&M costs. These costs and examples of how they are funded are described on p. 45.

Links to government schemes

From 1992 to 2003 village water supplies were funded with money from donor agencies. In 2003, when the GoI's *Swajaldhara* scheme was introduced, Gram Vikas decided to leverage government grants for rural water supply rather than continue depending on donor funds. However, the release of government funds seldom coincided with when the village needed them and this often caused delays in the construction of water towers. To address this problem Gram Vikas has recently reached an understanding with the government: now the District Water and Sanitation Mission, the village and Gram Vikas can enter into a tripartite agreement that enables Gram Vikas to pre-finance water-supply construction until the *Swajaldhara* funds are released, at which time Gram Vikas is reimbursed. It is hoped that this new understanding will reduce delays in construction.

Gram Vikas has also tried to leverage government grants under the GoI's TSC scheme. However, it has not been completely successful in this regard to date. In order to qualify for the subsidy a householder must be BPL, and the toilet must cost no more than INR2,000 in total. Each state government has its own way of interpreting the rules of the TSC, and it seems that each official also has his own interpretation of the state's TSC rules. Most of the villagers that Gram Vikas work with are genuinely BPL, but if an official wants to make an issue about handing over the grant it is easy for him to say: 'Your villages were covered before the TSC was launched in our district', or 'Your toilets are costing INR8,000–9,000.' As a result of conducting a lot of lobbying at state and district levels Gram Vikas has been successful in accessing the TSC subsidy in some districts of Orissa.

Financing by donors

External funding for Gram Vikas's RHEP work comes from a variety of sources, as shown in Table 7.2. The costs of running the organization and part of the programme expenses are supported by grants and donations from international institutions and individuals (around 90 per cent of annual costs). Programme interventions are also funded by the GoI, the Government of Orissa, and donations from Indian institutions and nationals (around 9–10 per cent of annual costs).

Gram Vikas receives international government funding from Switzerland (SDC), the UK (DFID), and the European Union (EU). It also receives funding from the following international NGOs: ICCO (Interchurch Cooperation), Netherlands; Christian Aid, UK; ADEME, France; BHP Billiton, London; Andheri Hilfe, Germany; CtxGrEen, Canada; SCIAF (Scottish Catholic International Aid Fund); Catholic Relief Services, US; Karl Kubel Stiftung, Germany; Rajiv Gandhi Foundation, India; NORAD, Netherlands; and EED, Germany.

Christian Aid, ICCO and the EU are the main donors to the RHEP. SDC has funded capacity training. Donor money also funds the social-cost subsidy that Gram Vikas gives to villagers (this subsidy is explained on pp. 33–4.

Table 7.2 Sources of external funding for the RHEP, in INR

	Indian			Foreign		Total
	Government	Institutional	Individual	Institutional	Individual	
Grants	8,024,843	33,333	0	79,399,681	0	87,457,857
Donations	0	0	454,755	47,361	390,948	893,064
% total	9.1	0.0	0.5	89.9	0.4	88,350,921

Source: Gram Vikas (annualized, based on figures for 2003–6).

CHAPTER 8
Generalizing the approach and scaling up

This final chapter considers the possibility of scaling up the RHEP approach, the external funds that would be required to do this for a sample figure of 100,000 households. The need to influence the government's policy on rural services, and how Gram Vikas proposes to do this, is looked at.

Scaling up Gram Vikas's approach to sanitation

'What began for Gram Vikas as single prong energy and environment initiative – 'the biogas' – has ... developed into a poverty alleviation program impacting the total quality of life of the marginalised rural population in Orissa. [Scaling-up] is important not only for Gram Vikas, but also for all participants in development initiatives at large, as the RHEP is an important sustainable development model worthy of replication.' (SDC, 2000)

Figure 8.1 illustrates the growth in the total number of households covered by the RHEP up to early 2007. From this it is clear that exponential growth is being experienced. Gram Vikas says that, although its very strict norms have meant that progress has been neither fast nor easy, its experience has shown that compromise can be costly and reduces the effectiveness of the programme. Villagers have gradually come to realize the merits of the approach, and today they themselves are the ambassadors of the programme. Demand, which was initially low, has greatly increased. Because the RHEP is based on people's involvement and initiative, Gram Vikas has been able to withdraw from practical control of day-to-day activities to periodically providing strategic direction. This hands-off approach has enabled its workers to cover nearby villages simultaneously. As almost 27,000 families in 362 villages spread the word across 19 districts, Gram Vikas expects to be able to reach 100,000 families by 2010 – around 1 per cent of the projected population of Orissa at that time (see Table 8.2 for a breakdown of the number of households to be covered each year). This is feasible when one takes into account the 'pull' of the demonstration effect of RHEP villages, and the assistance that other like-minded NGOs can give (see below).

Gram Vikas's longer-term aim is to cover 100,000 families every year from 2015 and reach a total of 1 million families (around 5 million people) – 12 per cent of the population of Orissa – by 2020.

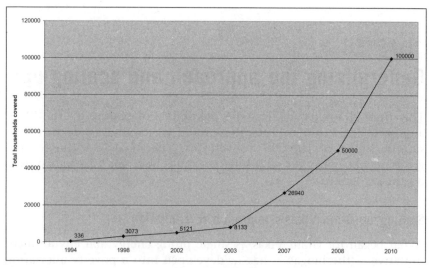

Figure 8.1 Households covered by the RHEP: actual and proposed
Source: Gram Vikas.

The RHEP approach is replicable: if the marginalized, chronically poor villagers of Orissa (who have been freely practising open defecation for centuries) are willing to pay the relatively high cost, then it is likely that the rural poor in most countries will also do so. To achieve 100 per cent consensus there must be clear boundaries to the extent of the community involved; this would seem to infer that the approach could not be so readily applied in urban or peri-urban districts. It can be assumed that the approach would have most rapid success in states surrounding Orissa because of the demonstration effect, but it should be transferable to other parts of India, Bangladesh, Pakistan, Nepal and Sri Lanka at least. Gram Vikas's experience shows that when the approach is adopted in a new location it takes some time to get off the ground, though use of a motivational film to illustrate the benefits certainly seems to help speed up consensus-building. In some countries a different sanitation technology may need to be offered but, in general, it should be possible to effectively apply the basic programme approach beyond Orissa.

Working with partner NGOs

Gram Vikas is increasingly networking with other small and medium-sized rural development NGOs in Orissa (Samajik Seva Sadan, ASSART, HELPLINE, WIDA, RAD, SWORD, Utkal Mani Seva Samiti, BISWA, MDDPPA), and other states in India. This alliance with other NGOs has been happening for about two or three years. The aim is that, by drawing on the experience of Gram Vikas, these partner organizations will be able to implement the RHEP model in their areas. Gram Vikas frequently hosts exposure visits of villagers and delegations from other NGOs, and in 2006 organizations from Orissa and out-of-state organizations (from Maharashtra, Jharkhand, Rajasthan and New Delhi, for instance) started to visit RHEP villages in Ganjam district. Some have already started to implement the RHEP, for example Magan Sangralaya Samiti in Wardha district of Maharashtra, and CYSD in Orissa. (It is interesting to note that Wardha is the district in which Gandhi had his ashram, and from which he advocated that India needed sanitation more urgently than it needed independence.) To date none of these partner NGOs have yet completed construction of the toilets and bathing rooms in a village; they are still on the preparatory/motivational phase.

External funds required for scaling up

The MDGs have raised the profile of water and sanitation in the fight against poverty, so it is reasonable to assume that these days it should be easy for NGOs working in the sector to raise funds for their work. However, although many billions of dollars have been promised to developing countries to assist them in meeting the MDGs, not much of the money gets to where it is needed. Gram Vikas says that the MDGs have made it no easier for them to get funding.

In order to reach out to significantly more communities, enormous amounts of additional funding are required. Gram Vikas estimates that the cost per household of implementing water supply and sanitation under the RHEP in the coming years will be in the order of US$700 (see Table 8.1). As time passes, and the habitations with good electricity supplies and water sources are serviced, it will become more costly to construct fully functional running-water supply systems; this extra cost has been factored into the figures. It is unlikely that beneficiaries will be able to support this extra cost which, under current *Swajaldhara* rules, will not be paid by the GoI, so external funding will be required. Of the US$700 cost per household for the RHEP, Gram Vikas estimates that it will need to source US$300 from donors. Applying this figure of US$300 to Gram Vikas's scaling-up proposal, it can be seen from Table 8.2 that the NGO will require US$30m in donor funding to cover 100,000 households in the four-year period from 2007 to 2010.

Table 8.1 Projected cost, in US$, per household to implement water and sanitation

Particulars	Cost	Donor funds required
Toilet, bathing room and three taps	200	100
Water supply and distribution system	400	100
Capacity building (5 yrs)	100	100

Source: Gram Vikas.

Table 8.2 Donor funds required to implement water and sanitation to 2010

	2007	2008	2009	2010	Total
Households covered in year	10,000	20,000	30,000	40,000	100,000
Total cost (US$m)	7	14	21	28	70
Donor funds required (US$m)	3	6	9	12	30

Source: Gram Vikas.

Influencing government policy

'Working with the poor requires political championing – the poor often have little visibility and relatively little voice. The key problem is not how to include the poor, but how to persuade stakeholders at *all* levels to do so.' (Deverill et al., 2002: 2, emphasis added)

Although the poor have 'relatively little voice', Gram Vikas realizes the importance of getting them to use that voice. Only when a community is united and its spirit raised will people demand from local government what is rightfully theirs. Gram Vikas has a limited capacity as an implementing body and can only ever make a tiny impact on the state as a whole. The challenge is how to make itself relevant to the bigger picture. This is already partly being done through working directly with other NGOs within and outside the state, but only the government has the capacity to institute change on a large scale. Gram Vikas can influence policy in favour of the poor by effective modelling and demonstration.

Gunyon states (1998: 26) that the government's strengths lie in creating policies to enable universal water and sanitation coverage. Those policies need to be 'consistently applied across government departments and throughout the different layers of government'. He says that India is in a good position (because of its well-developed NGO sector, the many small, low-income communities and the current large shortfall in sanitation coverage) to find out whether an imaginative use of government funds can enable communities to achieve their own facilities, or whether they will remain dependent on government agencies to provide them. The most effective way to increase sanitation coverage in India would be to get the government to adopt the idea of integrated water and sanitation development. Currently central (and state) government considers water and sanitation in isolation from each other; there is no integrated strategy, and for sustained health benefits they need to be integrated.

Gram Vikas has shown that, for maximum impact in empowering marginalized people, 100 per cent inclusion at all stages and the same good-quality facilities for all are important factors. These should be integrated into any government programme if empowerment and economic growth are to be achieved, not solely increased sanitation coverage. Gram Vikas makes big efforts to get government ministers and bureaucrats to visit RHEP villages; every little bit of exposure helps to spread the word about the long-term effectiveness of the programme. Government officers from other states have visited several villages in Ganjam district, including Samiapalli and Tamana. To increase its lobbying power, Gram Vikas is a member of the following state and national networks:

- ODAF (Orissa Development and Action Forum) – Orissa-level policy advocacy with a focus on tribal development
- PRIA (Society for Participatory Research in Asia) (an NGO working on governance issues, based in New Delhi) – national-level efforts directed towards strengthening grassroots level governance
- VANI (Voluntary Action Network, India) – bringing together diverse civil society actors at the national level, creating an enabling environment for promoting voluntary action
- INHAF – national-level habitat policy advocacy group
- Basin SA – national-level habitat policy advocacy group
- Credibility Alliance – NGO governance monitor

Gram Vikas also belongs to several international water-related networks: the Water Supply and Sanitation Collaborative Council (WSSCC), WASH (WSSCC's 'Water Sanitation and Hygiene for All' campaign) and the Freshwater Action Network (FAN), valuable forums for the exchange of information and lessons learned.

Advocacy and liaising with government are central to Gram Vikas's long-term funding strategy. Gram Vikas is involved in ongoing lobbying with the state and the central government in attempts to influence government policy on funding, particularly for the hardware costs of sanitation. The more costs the government bears, the less the dependency on donor funds. Exposure visits help to raise awareness of problems encountered with state government schemes and with delays in receiving funding. When government officials (state and national) see the RHEP water systems and the maintenance mechanisms, they appreciate that they are superior to the government's systems of handpumps and standpipes that rapidly fall into disrepair. When Gram Vikas first began working on water and sanitation projects the Government of Orissa did not view a piped water supply as a priority; it has since changed its outlook and now allows more opportunities to receive funds.

Gram Vikas wants to see the devolution of power regarding the implementation of water and sanitation projects to the local village level, the PRIs. To match that power, within the annual funding allocation to PRIs there should be sufficient funding to cover the social costs needed to implement the programme (as explained on pp. 33–4); if this were implemented rapid scaling up of sanitation coverage would be seen. *Palli sabhas* (the lowest-level PRIs, with members from each village) should control the sanctioning and release of these funds so that communities can effectively mobilize government resources to build the infrastructure they need, rather than having under-funded, poorly designed solutions thrust upon them.

Gram Vikas says that continued success of the RHEP will mean involving local government (block and GP) from the start of interventions in an area so that they will be encouraged to take ownership of the programme as it begins to show signs of success, and assist its expansion. Gram Vikas's aspiration to work with 1 per cent of the population of Orissa (100,000 families) by 2010, and 1 million households by 2020, is aimed at creating critical masses of people who are energized to seek their own development. By developing neighbouring villages so that clusters of empowered villagers will be formed, Gram Vikas is hoping to reach 20 per cent of the population in each of the GPs that are touched by the RHEP. They hope that this mass of mobilized people will be able to influence the workings of the PRIs (see Box 8.1).

Box 8.1 Jabana Bhuiyan: *panchayat* representative

'We used to weep within ourselves,' says Jabana Bhuiyan, of his childhood in Gira, a remote mountaintop tribal village. 'We ploughed, sowed and harvested under the hot sun, but went about empty-handed, with little to wear or eat.' A non-tribal landowner from another village exploited the villagers, taking most of the produce from every harvest.

Jabana became interested in working with Gram Vikas when he heard about the RHEP. He was trained as a mason and worked on the RHEP infrastructure for his village. Through this process he became confident and developed a strong rapport with the people of Gira. Encouraged by the success of his work, he became determined to build his awareness about problems facing his village and what could be done about them. By working with Gram Vikas he learned to read and write up to 3rd standard, his measurement, estimation and record-keeping skills improved and he learned to speak Oriya. He helped to educate others in his village by working as a facilitator.

In 1996, Gram Vikas encouraged Jabana and his friend, Alanda Mandal, to run for elected office as *panchayat* members. They made history in their area by becoming the first local people to be elected as representatives. For Jabana, winning or losing was not the issue: he had a mission to change the attitudes of people and help them broaden their expectations of what was possible.

Jabana knows about government schemes and programmes and how to implement government work orders through the village committees. He has succeeded in getting access to government medical facilities for the village and has obtained services in education, irrigation, roads and housing. Jabana now lives in nearby Karadasing, but frequently visits Gira, where he meets villagers, motivates and organizes village youth, and helps solve conflicts. He attends meetings and workshops and is cultivating good relationships with the government officials. He has ambitions of becoming a block chairman, district council member or member of the legislative assembly (MLA). Jabana's work is a source of happiness and satisfaction to him because – 'Things which seemed like a far-off dream are now a reality.'

Once people begin to experience managing their village water supply and sanitation systems, they begin to take an interest in the running of the *ward sabha* and *gram sabha*, the people's (registered voters') bodies at the lowest level of the PRI. The village general body is supported by Gram Vikas in formulating micro-plans for presentation in the *gram sabha*. Clustering the RHEP villages means that in any one *panchayat* there will be quite a few RHEP habitations. These villages together mount great pressure for the proper functioning of the *gram sabha* and hold to account the elected representatives of the GP. Similar efforts will be made to aggregate critical masses at the block, district and eventually state level. If enough people demand their rights to services and transparency in interactions the government must respond and put in place appropriate policies. Then communities will truly function as village republics, as envisaged by Gandhi.

Endnotes

1   A litre of water weighs 1 kg. The very basic quantity of water required for hygiene, drinking and cooking is estimated at 20 litres per person per day; when the round trip takes more than 30 minutes, people typically haul less water than they need to meet their basic requirements (WHO, 2006). For comparison purposes, households with private multiple-tap connections use 50–300 litres per person per day (washing-machines, dishwashers, power showers, car-washing, garden watering are all high consumers of water).

2   In Neeladripur village, in the Ganjam district of Orissa, women used to spend 5–6 hours per day fetching water. Now that they have running water in their houses they can use that time productively and thereby increase their family's income: they can earn INR5–7 per hour through broom-binding, brick-making or daily labour, all of which can add up to INR120–160 per week. Alternatively they might spend the time tending cash crops or working to otherwise increase the productivity of their fields.

3   In the five southerly states in which WaterAid supports projects (Andhra Pradesh, Karnataka, Maharashtra, Orissa and Tamil Nadu): 80 per cent of children suffer from waterborne disease each year and 28 per cent of child deaths are caused by diarrhoea and dehydration (Gunyon, 1998).

4   A village is considered 'fully covered' if it has a source within 1.6 km, one handpump for 250 people and 40 litres per day per adult (GoI, 2002b).

5   WaterAid–India (WAI, 2005: 22) make the point that it is difficult to verify water and sanitation coverage levels: although the Census of India does measure water (and sanitation) hardware, it does not assess the soft elements like the seasonality of the supply or the functionality of the source, and the same is true of the WHO/UNICEF/GoI study.

6   Two definitions of income poverty are commonly used in relation to India: the International Poverty Line (income per day equivalent to what US$1 would buy in the US), and the GoI's Official Poverty Line (income high enough for adequate nutrition). About 350 million Indians live below the former (DFID, 2006), and 260 million live below the latter.

7   In April 2006 the subsidy was raised from INR500 to INR1,200; however, the total TSC budget has not been increased proportionally, so there is likely to be a shortage of funding (WAI, 2006).

8   In Hindi (and Oriya), *gram* means village and *vikas* means development.

9   The organization now has 530 permanent staff and more than 600 volunteers in villages in 17 districts of the state. The head office is close to Berhampur (Brahmapur), in the southern part of the state.

10 Different districts in Orissa interpret the TSC regulations differently: some say that the RHEP toilets are much more expensive than the INR2,000 allowed for by TSC, and will not provide the subsidy (despite much lobbying by Gram Vikas); other districts are happy that the RHEP is complying with the spirit of the law and do provide the subsidy; still other districts insist that building stops at a certain wall height at which point they provide the subsidy, after that the building can resume. The subsidy, if given, goes directly to the BPL household: if that household has been assisted financially by the community the village general body may decide that the subsidy should go toward some community facility, such as a street light.

11 The length of time it takes to generate consensus depends upon how divided the village is: in some villages the leaders are able to generate the consensus without many meetings, but if the village is divided more meetings are needed. If a village really wants to join up it can come to consensus in one month. If a village is taking a long time (perhaps more than one year) to generate consensus, Gram Vikas withdraws until the villagers work it out. Learning to work out its problems is part of the community's development process.

12 Gram Vikas's extension worker is not always female; some villages (e.g. tribal villages in western Orissa) are open to having a man from outside talk to women, and one of Gram Vikas's project coordinators in that region is particularly successful at mobilizing women. Other parts of Orissa (especially Ganjam district) are very conservative and only female extension workers are allowed to talk to women behind closed doors. It all depends on the attitudes in the village. Meetings between Gram Vikas's male workers and village women take place in public areas, like temple grounds or the village meeting place.

13 Government regulations stipulate that SHGs consist of only 10–15 members of similar class/caste, so as to make a harmonious group

14 Gram Vikas has RHEP villages in most districts now; the furthest that a villager is likely to have to travel for an exposure visit is 80 km.

15 *100%* is a film in which people from 15 villages across four districts in Orissa – all at different points in the RHEP project cycle – talk candidly about their initial doubts and their experiences of the programme. Gram Vikas also shows villagers another film, *The Samantrapur Story,* which shows the reality of implementing the RHEP from start to finish, and the processes involved.

16 Wealthier households may opt to pay extra for a sanitary platform which incorporates footrests (as opposed to having separate footrests), and may spend more money on decorating their toilet or bathing room, but essentially the facilities are the same.

17 When the RHEP is being implemented the elderly and infirm build the same toilet facilities as everyone else. Gram Vikas's view is that it is important to first get people accepting the idea of sanitation without introducing too many new ideas at once, and the position adopted for the Indian-style toilet

is the same as that for open defecation, so it is probably the easiest toilet for people to adapt to. When people are familiar with using the Indian-style toilet the next step could be to introduce the western-style raised pedestal, which uses a sitting rather than a squatting pose and is therefore an easier position for the infirm.

18 Solar power equipment is very costly and only attracts a small subsidy from the government; also it does not provide enough power for larger villages in winter months. Gram Vikas is assisting with research into biodiesel for direct pumping, and both biodiesel and micro-hydro for generating electricity. Its current thinking is that these technologies are still too technical and uneconomic to be sustainable long-term for water supply in the RHEP villages.

19 *Swajaldhara* normally funds 90 per cent of the capital cost of a water supply, but that is for a lower level of service than that provided by the RHEP. The difference in cost for the increased level of service is paid for by the community.

20 The pilot phase was carried out in two districts: Ganjam district: Samiapalli (76 households), Sarakimpa (80) and Gobudi (46); and Bargarh district: Gouditikra (110) and Banhartikra (25).

21 Gram Vikas had contributed the remaining 55 per cent in cash.

22 Gram Vikas assists villagers in applying for funds until they feel confident enough to do it for themselves, but villagers themselves decide what improvements they want to make to their community.

23 Gram Vikas recognizes that the caste system is deeply ingrained in society; villagers only overcome it for RHEP purposes because they must do so in order to get water.

24 Most times the interest accruing every month is all that the villager can pay, making him almost a bonded slave of the moneylender.

25 A green-brick moulder working with the VSBK earns INR200–240 per 1,000 bricks, whereas the open market rate is as low as INR70 per 1,000 bricks. Usually the whole family is engaged in green-brick moulding, and a family moulds nearly 1,000 bricks per day. Brick-moulding is conducted in the colder months between November and February, because in hotter months the bricks would crack.

26 It is of course possible that improvements in health may be due to influences other than the RHEP, like other NGO initiatives or localized government schemes; however, other influences are unlikely to affect all villages in all districts, so by taking an overall view of villagers' health the statistical effect of any such external influence can be ignored.

27 Mackinnon (2002: 5) found child malnutrition to be 'slightly better' in Orissa than in the rest of the country.

28 Mackinnon (2002: 5) found child mortality to be worse in Orissa than in the rest of the country, and infant mortality (mortality in the first year) was officially estimated at 96 per 1,000 in 1997, compared with 71 per 1,000 in the rest of the country. No data after 1998 were available to Mackinnon.

29 Jaundice may be caused by hepatitis A infection, among other things (including AIDs). Hepatitis A infections are often due to contaminated water or food; a reduction in incidences of jaundice may therefore result from improved hygiene and sanitation.

30 The group discussions were conducted in June 2006. The findings have been reported independently in partial fulfilment of the author's Masters degree (Keirns, 2006).

31 During recent remodelling work on their toilets, men from Tamana village discovered that they are no longer happy to defecate outside: 'After so many years of using the toilet I can't do it outside anymore, it is terrible!'

32 Up to recently, if this issue was preventing 100 per cent consensus in a village, Gram Vikas would not implement the RHEP. Gram Vikas now takes the following approach: if a wealthy person refuses to join the RHEP it ignores him and continues to work with the rest of the people in building the infrastructure. As soon as the wealthy man sees that his servant's wife does not have to fetch water, or does not go outside to defecate, he will want to join the RHEP. At that point neither Gram Vikas nor the village committee will need to provide him with a subsidy; he will be willing to build his facilities at his own cost.

APPENDIX 1
The caste system

Hinduism and caste are interlinked. Hinduism is the product of a religious heritage that is 3,000 years old; it is a way of life, with complex rituals relating to many aspects of life, for example the food one can eat, how one should wash oneself, whom one should marry (Milner, 1994). The Hindu concept of rebirth is at the root of the acceptance by many Indians of a miserable existence: 'If a man suffers, it is his punishment for misdeeds in a former life, the penalty for breaking codes of Hindu behaviour and not the fault of a corrupt system' (Baker, 1990: 41). If one is to escape from the cycle of rebirth it is especially important to conform to one's *svadharma* (the rules and actions appropriate for one's own caste). Religious texts repeatedly remind the Hindu that it is more meritorious to perform one's own *svadharma* poorly than to perform another's perfectly.

Milner (1994) says that the origins of caste are obscure, but whatever the exact origin, by the 4th century BC the system was firmly entrenched. According to the classical religious Hindu texts the population is divided into four ranked categories called *varnas*: 1) Brahman (priest), today many Brahmans are preachers and teachers; 2) Kshatriya (warrior), today many join the army or police force, or become rich and influential landlords; 3) Vaisya (farmer, merchant) today many are businessmen, moneylenders and land-owners; 4) Sudras (labourer, servant), whose duty is to serve the three higher *varnas*; today these are officially known as the Backward Classes and they account for nearly a third of the Indian population, broken up into thousands of sub-castes with specific roles such as carpenters, weavers, blacksmiths, shepherds, potters and dhobis (washermen). In addition to these four categories, there are the Untouchables, who are outside the *varna* system but in fact are an integral part of the caste system. Alternative names for this group, who perform the most menial and degrading jobs (e.g. sweeper, sewage remover, handler of dead animals, bonded labourer), are *dalit* (Oppressed or Downtrodden), *harijan* (Children of God) and Scheduled Caste (SC). Though many Sudras compete with *dalits* for employment as labourers, they are not inclined to identify with the *dalit* lifestyle. There are very real, tangible advantages to being even a landless Sudra as compared with being a *dalit*.

It is unknown, says Milner, whether castes actually developed out of *varnas*, but the *varna* scheme has long served as a simplified indigenous model of the caste system. The actual society is organized into thousands of specific castes that are each associated with a traditional occupation. Only in a few of the artisan and service castes do most members earn their living from their traditional occupation, though in rural areas more members would at least occasionally perform their traditional functions. The caste structure in a given local area is composed of a small proportion of all of the possible caste categories. In most villages the number of castes represented ranges from 5 to 25. There are nearly always some type of Brahman and a variety of Sudra castes in a local area (though not necessarily in each village); in many areas the Kshatriya or Vaisya *varnas* are not present as their role has been taken over by Sudras. In most regions Untouchables make up at least 10 per cent of the population, and typically none of the top three *varnas* make as much as 10 per cent; so the bulk of the population are Sudras or some mix of Sudras and Untouchables.

The notion of purity is a central theme in Indian culture and, as a simplification, the gradations in the caste system and status are based on gradations of purity and impurity. Higher castes are purer than lower castes and must follow a lifestyle that conforms to the norms of purity if they are to maintain their superiority; many Brahmans will avoid physical contact with the lowest *dalits*. Many of the rules governing relationships between individuals and groups are rooted in this notion of purity and it shapes many of the daily activities, especially those to do with cooking, eating, personal cleanliness, dress, how one pays a visit, goes on a journey, makes conversation and worships. Conformity to the norms relating to purity is an important determinant of a local caste's status. For example, a caste that is vegetarian does no manual labour, prohibits its widows from remarrying, drinks no alcohol, carefully regulates the behaviour of its unmarried women and is fastidious about the observance of religious rituals: this is defined as living a relatively pure lifestyle. Accordingly, it has a higher status – other things being equal – than a caste that does not conform to this pattern. The rules that define purity and impurity vary somewhat from one locality to another, says Milner, but they are important in most parts of India. If one associates with those of lower caste, especially in intimate relationships such as eating and marriage, this will lower one's status; perhaps more significantly it also affects the status of other members of your family and caste. 'To break away from one's caste often means breaking from one's own family and group' (Baker, 1990: 53), and the resulting ostracism can only be survived by those of great courage or with the means to make a life away from their society.

For the overwhelming majority of people, caste is inherited at birth and in principle cannot be changed. The members of a particular caste in a village are linked to those in other villages by ties of kinship and marriage, forming regional caste units (sometimes referred to as sub-castes) ranging in size from a few hundred to perhaps tens of thousands (Milner, 1994). A regional sub-caste is a network of relatives or potential in-laws; members know each other directly or through trusted third parties. Usually husbands and wives are from the same sub-caste (or closely allied ones of similar status), and their children will also be members. 'Endogamy is the essence of the caste system, if there were no restrictions on cross-caste marriage, the caste system would cease to exist.' Accordingly, the vast majority of marriages are arranged by the parents.

In rural India *dalits* seldom use the same water source as the upper castes, says Baker (1990: 54): 'location of dwellings may partly explain this, but inherently no *Harijan* will seek out trouble from a caste Hindu, so dependent is he economically on his patronage'. In desert areas where *dalits* have asserted their rights by insisting on drawing water from the communal well, Brahmans have been known to send a camel to fetch water from a well some miles away, to avoid polluting themselves.

Milner says that there is some correlation between caste rank and economic and political power. Variations in the economic and political fortunes of upper and middle castes have probably always existed; some Brahmans are very rich and some are very poor. Drastic upward or downward movements are uncommon for the artisan castes, and rare for the lowest castes, especially the Untouchables. Typically, local political and economic structures are mainly controlled by a dominant land-owning caste or coalition; in most areas these controllers of land and labour are Sudras, not Brahmans. Social status is often represented by spatial distance in society, says Milner: in public gatherings higher-caste persons will tend to sit on a charpoy, or raised location, while lower-caste members will squat down; in the layout of villages the lowest-status groups are relegated to the margins of the settlement area; in the layout of temples the areas become increasingly sacred as one moves toward the inner sanctum; in the layout of homes the kitchen is the most pure and restricted area, while bedrooms, courtyards and latrine areas steadily increase in impurity and accessibility to outsiders.

Non-Hindus make up about 17 per cent of the Indian population: Muslims constitute about 11 per cent, and Sikhs, Christians, Jains and other minorities about 6 per cent, though the percentage in any given area varies enormously. Although caste-like features in these non-Hindu groups are much less elaborate than for Hindus, there is often a strong tendency for marriages to be arranged only between social strata that are fairly close to one another in rank.

Women's status in rural Indian society

Under the Indian constitution, theoretically women and men should enjoy equal status in every respect, and equal pay for equal work. In reality, however, the story is different. Patriarchy (i.e. male authority over the family) and patrilineal inheritance (i.e. the transmission of property and status via the male line) are features of Indian society; Milner (1994) says that the intensity of these patterns varies by region and caste. Few women, apart from midwives and teachers, have contact with others outside their own caste. In rural families, females suffer a subordinate position: 'In general women have very little control over land and other productive assets – this inequality in property rights directly contributes to women's low status in their families and the society' (Ghosh, 2006: 127). Ghosh studied one district in rural West Bengal. The findings of the study are not necessarily true for all of rural West Bengal, never mind all of rural India, but it gives a generalized picture of women's status in rural society.

Rural females generally have less access to education than males: in the state of West Bengal in 2001 the female literacy rate was lower than the male literacy rate (53.8 per cent compared with 73.7 per cent) (Ghosh, 2006: 111). Ghosh quotes the *West Bengal Human Development Report* of 2004 as saying that women of labouring households (both in agriculture and non-agriculture) are the worst off among the rural population in terms of illiteracy. Girl children are looked on as a burden in poor families: in most of India girls leave their parental homes on marriage and become members of a new family (Milner, 1994: 127). Boys are considered more desirable because they stay with the family and offer parents security in old age. Consequently girls may get less food and their education may be neglected. Girls are also often seen as a burden because a dowry must be supplied. Ghosh states that 44 per cent of West Bengali women had a body mass index (BMI) below the cut-off mark of chronic energy deficiency. The low earning capacity of rural families is an important factor in women's low protein (fish, meat or eggs) consumption, but intra-household distribution of food is also an important factor. Traditionally women take their meals after male members of their families so it is very rarely that women get enough. To change this ingrained practice, Ghosh says, both men's and women's awareness needs to be raised, and also women need to participate in the workforce so that both can contribute to the family purse.

Ghosh reports that only 40–55 per cent of women in rural West Bengal were in the workforce, mainly in agriculture as labourers or produce processors, areas requiring little skill and entrepreneurship. The majority of women have to hand over any earned income to the heads of their families (mostly men); they have no autonomy to save for themselves and for their future. Women also have to defer to the male heads of household regarding most of the economic activities within the household, not having control of household funds and little scope to exercise their views in decision-making regarding expenditure. 'Males dominate everywhere, whether women of their families earn income or women depend on men for sustenance' (Ghosh, 2006: 124).

Early marriage leads to early motherhood and the burden of a large family. Ghosh found there to be strong correlation between the level of education of girls and their age at marriage. The legal minimum marriage age for girls in India is 18 (for boys it is 21), but Ghosh found the mean age at marriage was well below 18, and in general areas with a high female literacy had a higher mean age at marriage. Ghosh also found that rural West Bengali women have very little choice and control in deciding when to have a child and in determining family size. The coverage of family-planning programmes is inadequate in rural areas of West Bengal, thus deepening the risk of repeated pregnancy. Ghosh quotes the *West Bengal Human Development Report* of 2004 as saying that around 30 per cent of births in rural areas were unplanned, while in urban areas 25 per cent were unplanned. To control population size it is important that women have greater control in family-planning decisions. Milner (1994) raised another marriage issue relating to women's status: remarriage of widows is still rarely permissible in the higher castes – the woman is considered by society to be 'jinxed' in some way and to be avoided. This taboo causes great hardship for a young bride if her husband dies before she has produced children.

Ghosh says that 'rural women have neither choice nor voice, but to accept the fact that they are women', and that 'education or employment only is not the panacea of all evils'. To enhance women's autonomy, she says, it is necessary to raise the awareness level of rural women, enabling them to form SHGs for social and economic purposes to get access and control over resources, providing support for challenging traditional norms which lead to gender inequity. 'It is expected that a large number of women members in all three tiers of the *panchayats* can play a meaningful role in ameliorating the miseries of women' (Ghosh, 2006: 130).

APPENDIX 3

Typical sanitation hardware used in rural areas of developing countries

Sanitation, for the purposes of this publication, refers to the safe management of human excreta through latrines ('hardware') and hygiene promotion ('software'). For most excreta-related infections, an improvement in excreta disposal must be accompanied by improved personal hygiene if they are to be controlled. It is also important that babies' excreta is disposed of safely and the baby's bottom is thoroughly cleaned after defecation.

Sanitation hardware in the context of low-income communities in developing countries usually means a toilet with an on-site disposal system, built on the owner's land, at his expense and frequently with his (or her) own hands (Cairncross and Feachem, 1993). The conventional cistern-flushed sewered systems used in developed regions of the world have a very high water demand to ensure that wastes are flushed off-site along the pipes; they are also technically difficult to construct and require some form of sewage treatment plant. The capital cost and O&M costs associated with these systems are generally considered too prohibitive for developing countries to adopt them on a large scale.

The health of the whole family depends on the use of latrines by people of all ages, including children who are old enough. Children under 10 years old are the main sufferers from excreta-related infections; they are also the main excreters of the pathogens that cause these diseases. Therefore, to encourage their use, it is important that children and the less able-bodied feel safe whilst squatting over a latrine. It is essential that latrines are kept clean, since a dirty latrine may cause more transmission of helminths (on feet/footwear) than would occur if people were to defecate in widely scattered locations in the open.

Many latrines do not meet minimal public health requirements, are not accessible to children, or are liable to pollute nearby wells. Waste pits are always accompanied by the danger of polluting water sources, particularly wells located nearby, and also water mains with low pressure. However, the risk of groundwater pollution is not necessarily a reason to reject on-site methods of human waste disposal. It is usually cheaper to provide an off-site water supply than off-site (sewered) sanitation.

A brief description of the sanitation hardware commonly used in rural areas in developing countries and options for low-cost improvements, follows, extracted from Cairncross and Feachem (1993).

Pit latrine

The simplest pit latrine is a hole in the ground over which the user squats, commonly with the feet on two planks of wood; a basic principle of this type of latrine is that fluids can seep into the ground. A simple superstructure of locally available materials can be built for privacy, with or without a roof. Disadvantages of this type of latrine are: 1) it smells; 2) flies often lay their eggs in faeces, and poorly built pit latrines can produce hundreds of flies carrying faecal pathogens on their bodies; 3) when the pit is full it must either be emptied so that the hole can be used again, or covered over with soil and a new pit dug. The former option has an attached health risk because pathogens, in particular roundworm eggs (*Ascaris*) and other helminths, are likely to be still viable and could cause disease transmission if strict hygiene practices are not observed.

The cheapest improvement to this type of latrine is to provide it with a prefabricated squatting slab or a seat: this makes the latrine safer to use (and it will *feel* safer, which is just as important to the user), less frightening for children and easier to clean. Incorporating footrests in the slab also makes it easier for people to position themselves correctly so the latrine does not become fouled. A tight-fitting lid may help to control flies and smell to some extent.

VIP latrine

The ventilated improved pit (VIP) latrine helps to reduce the smell and numbers of flies experienced in a conventional pit latrine. The essential improvements are the solid roofed superstructure and the vent pipe with mesh, which help to eliminate flies and effectively remove the smells emanating from the pit.

VIPs can have one or two pits. Where there are two pits, one is used for a given period (at least 12 months) until it is full, then the second pit is used. When the second pit is full the first is emptied and used again. In this way the excreta are never handled until at least 12 months old, when few, if any, *Ascaris* eggs will remain viable. Householders can empty their own pits by hand if they are able and keen to use the compost as fertilizer on their plots, and if the practice is acceptable to them; alternatively they can hire someone to do the job.

Pour-flush toilets

Adding a water seal, a U-pipe filled with water, below the squatting slab of a pit latrine will completely eliminate the problem of flies and odours. By using a shallow water seal the toilet can be efficiently flushed by pouring 1–3 litres of water down it (hence 'pour-flush'). To ensure that enough water is fetched for the toilet's operation the water supply needs to be close by. The small quantities of water used in a pour-flush toilet are enough to carry the waste to a soak pit up to 8 m away, which is easier to empty than a pit directly underneath the squatting slab. It is better to have two pits which are used alternately, one outlet being blocked off.

Pour-flush toilets are particularly suitable where water is used for anal cleansing, and they are very common in southern and southeastern Asia. If desired, the toilet can be located inside the house (upstairs or downstairs), and it can be upgraded to a cistern-flush toilet relatively easily.

References

Asian Development Bank (ADB) (2006) *Serving The Rural Poor: A Review of Civil Society-Led Initiatives in Rural Water and Sanitation* [online]. Asian Development Bank, Philippines. Available from: http://www.adb.org/Water/Topics/Rural-WSS/default.asp [accessed 29 August 2006].

Baker, S. (1990) *Caste: At Home in Hindu India*, Jonathan Cape, London, UK.

Cairncross, S. and Feachem, R. (1993) *Environmental Health Engineering in the Tropics: An Introductory Text,* 2nd edn, John Wiley & Sons, Chichester, UK.

Cardone, R. and Fonseca, C. (2006) 'Financing and Cost Recovery', Thematic Overview Paper, International Water and Sanitation Centre (IRC), Delft, The Netherlands[online]. Available from: http://www.irc.nl/page/7582 [accessed 16 August 2006].

Department for International Development (DFID) (2005) *Partnership for Development – DFID's Country Plan in India: State Plan for Orissa, 2004-2008* [online]. DFID, UK. Available from: http://www.dfidindia.org/pub/pdfs/cap_india.pdf [accessed 24 August 2006].

DFID (2006) *Asia Factsheet – India* [online]. DFID, UK. Available from: www.dfidindia.org [accessed 24 August 2006].

Department of Drinking Water Supply (DDWS) (undated) *Total Sanitation Campaign*, Delhi [online]. Available from: http://www.ddws.nic.in/tsc-nic/html/index.html [accessed 16 July 2006].

Deverill, P., Bibby, S., Wedgwood, A. and Smout, I. (2002) *Designing Water Supply and Sanitation Projects to Meet Demand in Rural and Peri-Urban Communities: Book 3: Ensuring the Participation of the Poor* [online]. Water, Engineering and Development Centre (WEDC), Loughborough University, UK. Available from: http://wedc.Lboro.ac.uk/ [accessed 24 March 2006].

de Wit, J. (2005) *A Cost-Benefit Analysis of the Community-Based Water Supply and Sanitation Program of Gram Vikas,* unpublished. Available from Gram Vikas: info@gramvikas.org

Gely, J. (2006) *Experiences with Strategic Planning for Rural Drinking Water and Sanitation in District Municipalities: PROPILAS II, a Pilot Project to Improve District Water and Sanitation Management and Sustainability* [online]. Water and Sanitation Program-Latin America and the Caribbean, Peru. Available from: http://www.wsp.org/publications/propilas.pdf [accessed 16 July 2006].

Ghosh, D.K. (2006) 'Women's autonomy in rural West Bengal: a case study', *Journal of Rural Development* (quarterly of the National Institute of Rural Development, Hyderabad, India) 25: 103–30.

Government of India (GoI) (2002a) *10th Five-Year Plan (2002–2007), Vol. II Sectoral Policies and Programmes* [online]. Planning Commission, Government of India. Available from: http://planningcommission.nic.in/plans/planrel/fiveyr/10th/default.htm [accessed 13 August 2006].

GoI (2002b) *India Assessment 2002: Water Supply and Sanitation* [online]. Planning Commission, Government of India. Available from: http://planningcommission.nic.in/reports/genrep/wtrsani.pdf [accessed 12 August 2006].

GoI (2005) *Mid-Term Appraisal of the 10th Five-Year Plan (2002–2007): Water Resources* [online]. Planning Commission, Government of India. Available from: http://planningcommission.nic.in/midterm/english-pdf/chapter-06.pdf [accessed 12 August 2006].

Gram Vikas (2003a) *100%, The Samantrapur Story* (motivational films). Available from: info@gramvikas.org

Gram Vikas (2003b) *Summary Report of RHEP Phase 1 Household Survey*, unpublished. Available from: info@gramvikas.org

Gram Vikas (2006a) Author's interviews with Gram Vikas employees, conducted in June 2006 at its head office in Mohuda, Orissa.

Gram Vikas (2006b) *Annual Report 2005–06* [online]. GramVikas, Berhampur, Orissa. Available from: http://www.gramvikas.org/ [accessed 30 October 2006].

Gram Vikas (2007) 'History and Evolution'. Available from: http://www.gramvikas.org/ [accessed 5 June 2007].

Gunyon, W. (1998) *India: Making Government Funding Work Harder* [online]. WaterAid, London, UK. Available from: http://www.wateraid.org/documents/indgovfund.pdf [accessed 24 May 2006].

Jackson, B. (2004) *Sanitation and Hygiene in Kenya: Lessons on What Drives Demand for Improved Sanitation*, Field Note, Water and Sanitation Program–Africa, Nairobi, Kenya.

Jenkins, M.W. and Curtis, V. (2005) 'Achieving the good life: why some people want latrines in Rural Benin', *Social Science & Medicine* 61: 2446–59.

Kar, K. (2003) *Subsidy or Self-Respect?: Participatory Total Community Sanitation in Bangladesh* [online]. Institute of Development Studies (IDS), Brighton, UK. Available from: http://www.ids.ac.uk/ids/bookshop/wp/wp184.pdf [accessed 18 March 2006].

Keirns, P. (2006) *Community Empowerment: A Case Study of Gram Vikas' Water and Sanitation Work in Rural Orissa, India*, unpublished MSc research project, WEDC, Loughborough University, UK.

Maharashtra Water Supply and Sanitation Department (MahaWSSD) (undated) *Inventive Villagers: Innovative Approaches to Total Sanitation in Maharashtra* [online]. Government of Maharashtra Water Supply and Sanitation Department. Available from: http://www.mahawssd.gov.in/prjInnov.asp?innovid=132 [accessed 16 July 2006].

Majumdar, J. (1994) 'Policy/Strategy for Action: Finance', in *Ministerial Conference on Drinking Water and Environmental Sanitation Implementing UNCED Agenda 21*, Netherlands Minister of Housing, Physical Planning and Environment (VROM), Noordwijk, The Netherlands.

Mackinnon, J. (2002) *Assessing the Impact of Fiscal and Structural Reforms on Poverty in Orissa* [online]. DFID, Delhi. Available from: http://www.odi.org.uk/prspsynthesis/India(Orissa)_Final_PSIA.doc [accessed 22 July 2006].

Milner, M. (1994) *Status and Sacredness: A General Theory of Status Relations and an Analysis of Indian Culture*, Oxford University Press, New York.

Moriarty, P. and Butterworth, J. (2003) *The Productive Use of Domestic Water Supplies: How Water Supplies can play a Wider Role in Livelihood Improvement and Poverty Reduction* [online], Thematic Overview Paper, International Water and Sanitation Centre (IRC), Delft, The Netherlands. Available from: http://www.irc.nl/page/3733 [accessed 23 August 2006].

Noor, T.R. and Ashrafee, S. (2004) 'An End to Open Defecation: Process, Cost, Motivation and Sustainability', in Sam Godfrey (ed.) *People-Centred Approaches to Water and Environmental Sanitation. 30th WEDC International Conference, Vientiane, Lao PDR, 2004*, pp. 120–3, Water, Engineering and Development Centre (WEDC), Loughborough University, UK.

Overseas Development Institute (ODI) (2002) *Poverty Reduction and Water: 'Watsan and PRSPs' in Sub-Saharan Africa*, Water Policy Brief no. 3 [online]. Overseas Development Institute, London. Available from: http://www.odi.org.uk/ [accessed 9 October 2006].

Swiss Agency for Development and Cooperation (SDC) (2000) *The RHEP Documentation*, unpublished study conducted by the Swiss Agency for Development and Cooperation (SDC). Available from: Gram Vikas: info@gramvikas.org

United Nations Children's Fund (UNICEF) (2006) 'Child mortality', UNICEF Statistics [online]. Available from: http://www.childinfo.org/areas/childmortality/u5data.php [accessed 16 August 2006].

WaterAid (undated) *Wider Impacts of Water, Sanitation and Hygiene Education Projects*, Issue sheet [online]. WaterAid, London. Available from: www.wateraid.org [accessed 24 November 2006].

WaterAid–India (WAI) (2005) *Drinking Water and Sanitation Status in India: Coverage, Financing and Emerging Concerns* [online]. WaterAid India, New Delhi. Available from: http://www.wateraid.org/documents/drinking_water_and_sanitation_status_in_india.pdf [accessed 24 May 2006].

WAI (2006) *Sanitation for the Poor—Still a Long Way to Go,* Country paper for the 2nd South Asia Conference on Sanitation (SACOSAN), Pakistan. WaterAid, India.

Water and Sanitation Program–South Asia (WSP–SA) (2002) 'Making Sanitation Work', *Jal Manthan* 7 [online]. Water and Sanitation Program–South Asia, New Delhi. Available from: http://www.wsp.org/publications/sa_jalmanthan7.pdf [accessed 24 March 2006].

WELL (2006) *Microfinance for Sanitation* [online]. Factsheet, WELL, Loughborough University, UK. Available from: http://www.lboro.ac.uk/well/resources/fact-sheets/fact-sheets-htm/mcfs.htm [accessed 16 July 2006].

World Bank (2003) *Strategic Approach for Sustainable Financing of Community Infrastructure in India*, Joint WorldBank/Department for International Development UK study for GoI, World Bank, New York.

World Health Organization (WHO) (2004) *Meeting the MDG Drinking-Water and Sanitation Target: A Mid-Term Assessment of Progress* [online]. World Health Organization, Geneva, Switzerland. Available from: http://www.who.int/ water_sanitation_health/monitoring/jmp2004/en/ [accessed 17 August 2006].

WHO (2006) *Meeting the MDG Drinking Water and Sanitation Target: The Urban and Rural Challenge of the Decade* [online]. World Health Organization, Geneva, Switzerland. Available from: http://www.who.int/ water_sanitation_health [accessed 7 November 2006].

Wiki (undated) 'Gram panchayat', Wikipedia [online]. Available from: http:// en.wikipedia.org/wiki/Gram_panchayat [accessed 20 August 2006].

Index